'If you want to understand how new technologies, in particular, artificial intelligence, will affect your career or business, this is the book for you. Somi Arian clearly explains the skills that you need to succeed in the 21st century.' CHRISTOPHE GEORGES, PRESIDENT AND CEO, BENTLEY

'Somi Arian's book is just what is needed right now as she examines the existential impact of technology and in particular AI on us all, individuals and businesses alike. Her approach is both philosophical and practical and will enable the reader to build the right mental and emotional toolset to navigate and thrive within the accelerating change and disruption. It's a must-read!' JUSTINE SOUTHALL, MANAGING DIRECTOR, MARIE CLAIRE JET STYLE, AND FORMER MANAGING DIRECTOR OF *MARIE CLAIRE*

'If, like me, you've consumed so much content on the "future of work" lately that you feel more agitated than up-to-date, read *Career Fear*. It's that signal in the noise I was searching for!' JACKIE BAREFIELD, HEAD OF LEARNING, BARCLAYS INTERNATIONAL

'Rapidly advancing technologies are disrupting our 21st-century careers and outmoding conventional career planning strategies. This book is a no-nonsense guide to cultivating and applying our uniquely human proficiencies – from ethics to emotional intelligence to contextual understanding – to achieving durable relevance in the face of an increasingly volatile job market.' DAN RUDERMAN PHD, DIRECTOR OF ANALYTICS AND MACHINE LEARNING, UNIVERSITY OF SOUTHERN CALIFORNIA

'Somi Arian does a great job of demystifying the forces that create a successful career in the post-digital revolution era.' MICHAEL O'TOOLE, FORMER MANAGING DIRECTOR AT MORGAN STANLEY

'As an HR professional, I am encouraging all to read this to understand better how AI will and is impacting career paths and skills development now and in the future. For all of those concerned by the large scale introductions of AI technology into the workplace, Somi Arian's book and narrative sets out the context and what differentiates us and how to continue to add value to yourself, your career and the organizations you work for mindfully and relevantly.' JACQUE FIELD, GLOBAL HEAD OF RESOURCING AND EMPLOYER BRANDING, VODAFONE

'Committing to lifelong learning and nurturing soft skills that are innately human are crucial for success in the post-digital era. Somi Arian inspires you to start your learning journey today and beautifully articulates the personal satisfaction and opportunity that can be unlocked by developing a growth mindset.' NAMRATA MURLIDHAR, MARKETING DIRECTOR, LINKEDIN LEARNING

'Somi Arian is bringing an actual and relevant perspective to the future of work, which is actually a reality to act on right *here* and *now*. Besides her book being a great guide for all of us on how to leverage new technologies in harmony and complementarity to our unique competencies, it is also an essential read for all leaders who would like to stay ahead of the curve and set their organization for success.' ALINA COJOCARU, LEARNING AND DEVELOPMENT MANAGER, THE LEGO GROUP

'This concise, well-structured, immensely readable book presents thoughtful analyses of the impact of technological and managerial developments on the nature of work, different types of careers, gaining the mindset to select an appropriate career and acquiring the human skills required to succeed in it. I recommend this book to ambitious early career professionals as well as everyone else seeking to secure their futures.' THOMAS W HARTQUIST, EMERITUS PROFESSOR OF ASTROPHYSICS, UNIVERSITY OF LEEDS

'It seems to me this is a very necessary book for this new era, driving you through an epiphanic journey about our ever-changing world context, from which we cannot escape, which we try to handle, and which is a key to our own selves in this complex path to succeed in life.' PATRÍCIA ÁLVARES, EDITOR IN CHIEF, SPUTNIK NEWS

'This book tackles the big issues for those entering the world of work. It offers practical advice about how to choose the right vocation so that readers can gain satisfaction and a decent income from their job.' LUKE JOHNSON, CHAIRMAN, RISK CAPITAL, AND FORMER CHAIRMAN OF CHANNEL 4

'Most career books are about the how – how to get a job, ace that interview or climb the career ladder. This book is about the why of work. It invites you to delve deeply into what work means to you, why you've chosen your job role and what work will look like in the future. The speed of career change means none of us knows where our career paths are heading, but this book is a step to making sense of work now and to the end of the century.' JANE HAMILTON, CAREERS EDITOR, THE SUN

'In Career Fear, Somi Arian has written a wonderfully readable, accessible guide to the future of work. It starts by explaining the profound changes that are already taking place in how people work and explores the opportunities to reimagine work that disruptive technologies, in particular, are bringing. The book then offers an inspiring argument about how we can re-humanize work and how, if we are smart and alert to what is happening, we can benefit hugely from human–machine relations by developing those skills which are unique to human beings: emotional intelligence, critical thinking, contextual creativity and mindfulness. For anyone who works with young people, this is a powerfully uplifting vision of what the world of work could become.' JONNIE NOAKES, DIRECTOR OF TEACHING AND LEARNING AT ETON COLLEGE AND DIRECTOR OF TONY LITTLE CENTRE FOR INNOVATION AND RESEARCH IN LEARNING

'If you want to get ready for the future of work, you need to read *Career Fear*! It focuses on one aspect of work that will not change: people. The dangerous judgement errors that we bring to the workplace because of how our brains are wired, called cognitive biases, will become even more problematic for us in the increasingly disrupted future. *Career Fear* will help you understand how to address these problems and succeed in the workplace of the future through equipping readers with key skills to get ready for the challenges to come.' DR GLEB TSIPURSKY, BESTSELLING AUTHOR AND CEO OF DISASTER AVOIDANCE EXPERTS

'This book is nothing short of amazing! Somi Arian's writing style is concise, easy to understand and so powerful. It pulled me in from the moment I started reading. It sums up pretty much what all of us in the modern workplace go through, and clearly states what we need to do about it. As a learning and development administrator in the corporate world today, and being in the corporate rat race for over 30 years, this subject resonates with me so much!' NICK LECHNIR, LEARNING AND DEVELOPMENT SYSTEM ADMINISTRATOR, LOGISTICS HEALTH INCORPORATED

'The pace of change doesn't just disrupt business, it has and will disrupt your career as well. Somi Arian wrote the book on future-proofing your career. It's not just about how to find a job, but about how all of us will find our way in the future of work.' DAVID BURKUS, BESTSELLING AUTHOR OF *UNDER NEW MANAGEMENT*

'The world of work is rapidly changing, but the instruments to understand it have remained stagnant. This is where *Career Fear* comes in. With an entertaining blend of data and storytelling, Somi Arian's book provides a timely, powerful and enriching perspective on this ever-changing landscape. Equal parts informative and practical, *Career Fear* will allow you to see the world of work with newfound clarity and will equip you with the tools to thrive within it.' MATT JOHNSON PHD, AUTHOR OF *BLINDSIGHT*, PROFESSOR OF CONSUMER NEUROSCIENCE AND NEUROMARKETING AT HULT INTERNATIONAL BUSINESS SCHOOL, TEDX AND KEYNOTE SPEAKER

Career Fear
(and how to beat it)

Get the perspective, mindset and skills you need to futureproof your work life

Somi Arian

KoganPage

Publisher's note

Every possible effort has been made to ensure that the information contained in this book is accurate at the time of going to press, and the publishers and authors cannot accept responsibility for any errors or omissions, however caused. No responsibility for loss or damage occasioned to any person acting, or refraining from action, as a result of the material in this publication can be accepted by the editor, the publisher or the author.

First published in Great Britain and the United States in 2020 by Kogan Page Limited

2nd Floor, 45 Gee Street	122 W 27th St, 10th Floor	4737/23 Ansari Road
London	New York, NY 10001	Daryaganj
EC1V 3RS	USA	New Delhi 110002
United Kingdom		India
www.koganpage.com		

Kogan Page books are printed on paper from sustainable forests.

© Somi Arian, 2020

ISBNs

Hardback	978 1 78966 465 2
Paperback	978 1 78966 462 1
Ebook	978 1 78966 463 8

British Library Cataloguing-in-Publication Data

A CIP record for this book is available from the British Library.

Library of Congress Cataloging-in-Publication Data

Names: Arian, Somi, author.
Title: Career fear (and how to beat it) : get the perspective, mindset and skills you need to futureproof your work life / Somi Arian.
Description: London, United Kingdom ; New York, NY, USA : Kogan Page Limited, 2020. | Includes bibliographical references and index. |
Identifiers: LCCN 2020007630 (print) | LCCN 2020007631 (ebook) | ISBN 9781789664652 (hardback) | ISBN 9781789664621 (paperback) | ISBN 9781789664638 (ebook)
Subjects: LCSH: Job security. | Job satisfaction. | Career development.
Classification: LCC HD5708.4 .A75 2020 (print) | LCC HD5708.4 (ebook) | DDC 650.1–dc23
LC record available at https://lccn.loc.gov/2020007630
LC ebook record available at https://lccn.loc.gov/2020007631

Typeset by Integra Software Services, Pondicherry
Print production managed by Jellyfish
Printed and bound by CPI Group (UK) Ltd, Croydon CR0 4YY

Contents

Introduction

Career success today looks *nothing* like it did a few decades back when our parents and grandparents were entering the job market. The truth is that so many of the career paths that were popular in the past may not exist in the not so far future. Even if they are still around in the next few years, they may look absolutely nothing like they do now. Machine learning algorithms are quickly chipping away at the tiny tasks that make up most jobs – who knows what jobs will be around in five years' time, even?

As if finding a job wasn't hard enough, we now have to think about finding the *right* job that's futureproof, too. So, what about you? What do you do for a living? Is it a job, a career – or even a calling? How do you know the difference?

With all of these questions, it's no wonder that career fear is so common!

Here's a little about my story; how I figured out how to tackle these questions. When I was a child in Tehran, I dreamed of becoming an astronaut, but I wasn't good enough at maths. Instead, I ended up majoring in philosophy of science and political theory, where the questions that kept me awake as a child became the driving force of a lifetime of work and research. I wanted to know who I was, why I was here, and how to be happy. Through searching for my own happiness and alleviation of suffering, I learnt that the only real way of finding happiness and fulfilment was by helping *others* find their happiness, and alleviating *their* suffering.

Through a lifetime of trial and error, I learnt what it takes to find a fulfilling career path that will make you happy. Find an area, in any field, where you can get really good at what you do, and help other people's problems or enhance the quality of their lives.

Congratulations... you now have a fulfilling career!

Of course, it's not that simple. I wish it were. First of all, it took me a *long* time to figure out that I should be focusing on what I can bring to the world, instead of single-mindedly pursuing happiness. But even after this fell into place for me, there's still another piece of the puzzle.

Know thyself

Something else I've discovered through seeking the answers to the questions I had as a child... you can't be happy and thrive in your life and career until you *know yourself*. Since the times of Ancient Greek philosopher Socrates, 'know thyself' has been the oldest advice in the book. But even Socrates himself didn't actually explain *how* to know yourself. What does it really mean and how do we do it? This is a problem, because I would argue that knowing yourself has never been more urgently needed than it is in our society today.

Arguably, the biggest challenge we face today is the pace of technological advancement. As digital natives, we are so used to the speed of change and constant stimulation from brands, social media platforms and internet gurus that it's hard to identify and focus on what's important.

The inherent property of speed is that it takes away your clarity. Imagine you are in the passenger seat of a car moving at 180 miles per hour, looking out of the window: it's hard to see much of what's on the side of the road, right? You can only begin to see things more clearly when the car slows down. Finally, everything looks completely clear when the vehicle stops.

We are like the passenger in the backseat of a car moving at 180 miles per hour. The speed of life in the age of digital technologies and artificial intelligence is blurring our vision. It doesn't leave us enough room to see the big picture, grasp the challenges ahead, and self-reflect. What we forget is that humans do not set this speed – algorithms set it.

Let's take peer pressure, for example. For our generation, peer pressure is very different from what it was like for the previous generations. It's no longer just about the neighbour's kid, or your cousin who went to Harvard.

Every day, we see social media images of entrepreneurs who seem to have it all at increasingly younger ages. In 2018, 62 per cent of digital natives had said that they wanted to be entrepreneurs. Of those who worked in companies, 35 per cent already had a side hustle.

We are reminded by successful entrepreneurs on social media that speed is the currency of our time. We need to act faster and work harder. You want to be a 20 under 20, a 30 under 30, or a 40 under 40! Who sets these deadlines? We are not all equal in our starting point. Is it realistic for people of diverse backgrounds to be compared by the same yardsticks of success? For years, I dealt with so much anxiety over not achieving specific career goals by self-inflicted deadlines. I was failing to take into consideration my physical conditions, my background as an immigrant, skin colour, accent, psychological makeup, gender, and many other factors.

I was born in one of the poorest neighbourhoods of Tehran and grew up during the war, in a hostile environment, plagued by prejudice and tradition. My parents disowned me at the age of 18. I taught myself English, and worked for the United Nations and diplomatic circles from the age of 19. I then moved to the UK in 2005, where I put myself through education, including a stint at St Andrews University. I managed to obtain two master's degrees in politics and philosophy, and worked as a TV producer in London for five years, before starting my own business.

I say this not to show off, or to try to make you feel even worse about yourself, but because the point is this: despite everything I had achieved, *I still felt like a complete failure.*

I endured *so much* unnecessary suffering in pursuit of a vague notion of success – I was letting my 'career fear' drive me, with no respect for what I had achieved and overcome. It wasn't until I gained clarity on the topics of this book that I started to see a glimpse of happiness and fulfilment. What is the point of career success if you don't feel fulfilled?

The key elements of beating career fear

Through self-reflection, research and years of experience, I learnt that there are three vital components to career success and fulfilment: perspective, mindset and (human) skills. Those key elements have always been important, but in today's world of technological disruptions, they find a whole new level of significance.

Admittedly, understanding them on an intellectual level isn't enough. Internalizing and putting them into practice is a lifelong process. In this book, we will look at each element in turn, and I will share my experience and methods with you, with some tips on how to apply what we're learning to your own life and beat your own career fear. Socrates said 'know thyself' – he didn't say how. This is a book that I wish I had had when I was starting.

PART ONE

Perspective

Everything that we do and say in life is a story. Every single conversation, text message, social media post, film or piece of news is a story. A compelling story has three parts to it: set-up (or context), conflict (or problem) and resolution (or answer).

Another critical aspect of storytelling is 'perspective'. Tolstoy said that there are only ever two stories: 'A man goes on a journey, or a stranger comes to town.' I would take this one step further and say that there is only ever one story – of course, the man that goes on a journey *is* the stranger that comes into town. The question is from whose perspective we tell a story.

This book is also telling a story, and so it has three parts to it:

- **The set-up**
  Disruptive technologies have entered and are entering our career landscape. We will look at this in Chapter 1.

- **The problem**
  We lack a proper framework, and mindset, for dealing with these technologies. We will explore this more in Chapter 2 – and start looking at practical solutions in Part Two, Mindset.

- **The resolution**
  We need to develop the right kind of skills for coping with disruptive technologies. Chapters 3 and 4 look forward to the future of work – and Part Three, (Human) skills, looks at some practical ways to develop those skills.

But first, we need to start with the right perspective – who's telling this story? The best way to gain perspective and see the context is by looking at the career landscape in the past, present and future, which is what we will do in the next four chapters.

CHAPTER ONE

A history of work

The concept of work, or its modern version 'career', has become such an essential aspect of our modern lives that it's hard to imagine a time when people didn't even have a word for work in their vocabulary. I find this particularly mind-blowing, because my personal relationship with work is a very close one – work, for me, is linked to my identity. Even if you are strongly in the work–life balance camp, chances are your work has a big impact on your sense of identity, too.

In this first chapter, we will look at a history of work: a whistle-stop tour of human beings and their 'jobs', 'careers' and attitudes towards work. For me, learning about the history of work is like a lightbulb moment; finally, everything makes sense, as you learn *why* we work and how it all began. Once we grasp where it came from, we can understand the most important thing for you and me: where is it going?

First, though, let's address the elephant in the room.

The question of work–life balance

There is a lot of discussion these days about 'work–life balance'. As I mentioned, work for me is closely tied to who I am – so much so, that for a long time, I didn't get why people insisted so much on separating 'work' and 'life'. Surely, work *was* life?! At least it seemed that way to me: some people can't wait for the weekend so that they can have a break, whereas I'm the kind of person who can't wait for the weekend so I can do my most creative work without interruption.

If you are a fan of books like *The 4-Hour Work Week* by Tim Ferris, you may be in the 'work–life balance' camp. This is the mindset that views work as mainly a source of income. Ferris – and many others like him – suggest that you should strive to minimize your work hours and maximize your income, preferably making it as passive as possible.[1]

What I'm about to say in this chapter may appear to be the exact opposite of this point of view. However, don't be too quick to judge. I'd argue that what I'm going to say isn't actually that far from Ferris' viewpoint at all. For example, some people may be inclined to say that I'm a workaholic. That's not how I see myself at all – but here's the point: what other people define as work, to me, is just *being*. I enjoy what I do so much that I don't separate work from leisure.

As I write these words, I'm on a short holiday in Portugal. I know that if I'm found typing on my computer for too long, my boyfriend will remind me to rest and enjoy my break. For me, a break is not separate from work, and work is not different from the pursuit of knowledge and growth. I'm the kind of person who would sit in a bubble bath and listen to an audiobook or an article from *The Economist* – grateful that they now make them available in audio format. Could you say that I'm having a break or working at that moment as I bathe? I consider my work as a calling: it's not a job to me, or even a career.

Work–life blend

And I'm not the only one. When you look at social media today, you will see that I'm not an anomaly. This attitude to work seems to be the standard way of life for many entrepreneurs, authors, scientists, content creators and artists. It has always been that way throughout history. Do you think, for example, that Mozart, Einstein, Nietzsche and Aristotle were concerned about work–life balance? I very much doubt it. But, of course, they didn't have the internet so they were unable to share their progress and excitement on Instagram and LinkedIn. I can imagine Einstein tweeting his thoughts as he developed his theory of relativity! Newton famously worked such long hours and immersed himself in his work so much that he once boiled his watch instead of an egg.

Here's what I believe, and what we'll look at more closely later on in this book: if you view work as a calling rather than merely a job, your attitude will change. You will be much more flexible and ready to learn and adapt to new technologies. You will naturally be inclined to find areas where you can contribute to society, have an impact and feel fulfilled. Most importantly, you will never compare yourself to others. It won't matter how successful other people may appear on social media. You will know who you are and what you can do.

All of this will become a lot easier and more interesting when you find your place in the world and get passionate about having a calling. To have a calling is to live life as a game. It is to enjoy the pain and the frustration of learning, growing, creating, failing, and starting all over again. It is not just a job, or just an income, or just a means to an end.

All of which raises the question: how did the value of work diminish to 'just a job' in the first place?

From early humans to the first disruptors

When I look at the history of work, what strikes me is a sense that humans have had a love–hate relationship with it. At least, this is the case in so far as we think of work as a means to feed and shelter ourselves.

In his excellent book *The History of Work*, Richard Donkin notes that, historically, the term work meant something to be avoided. It referred to what we might now describe as chores. In other words, from early history, work was viewed as a kind of burden. Ancient Greeks didn't even have a word for this action, Donkin says. They had words for leisure and learning, but nothing that directly defined the activity we now know as work.[2]

Perhaps one of the reasons for this is that most of the early history of work was based on slavery. Sadly, the further back we go into the depths of human history, the less information we have about how our ancestors lived: in his book *Sapiens*, Yuval Noah Harari explains that early humans' position in the food chain was in the middle. He describes a scenario where a lion would kill another animal: the lion and her family would eat the flesh; hyenas and other animals ate the remainder; and finally, humans were able to get to the middle of the carcass (the bone marrow). Humans did this using sharp tools that they created from stones and wood. This enabled them to access nutrients that were untouched by other animals, avoiding contamination.[3] We can think of this process as an early form of work. You can imagine why it wasn't exactly pleasant: you'd have to have a lot of patience hanging around until it was your turn to get to the food.

But of course, things moved on. As humans got more sophisticated at creating sharp tools, they were also able to kill smaller animals. Discovery of fire enabled them to cook previously indigestible foods. Access to these new kinds of nutrients was crucial in the growth and development of the human brain. As our brains developed, we also became more adept at using our hands to create tools and make fire and shelter. At the same time, humans started to stand upright and walk on two feet.

According to Harari, the combination of standing upright and the growth of the human brain came at a high cost, especially to women. Standing upright meant that women's hips got narrower over time, making childbirth much more difficult. This was just at a time when our brains were getting bigger. The combination of bigger brains and narrower hips in women has meant that children are born while most of their vital systems are still underdeveloped. In most other animals, their babies can stand on their feet and live independently much more quickly than humans. But human babies need the protection of their parents for many years before they can be independent.[4]

This evolutionary fact has had both positive and negative impacts on human evolution. Perhaps most relevant for this book was the need to create social bonds and contracts to be able to survive. From there, it's not hard to imagine how the concept of work was born: imagine a group of hunter-gatherers. While men were out in the wild in pursuit of meat, women looked for fruit, nuts and grains that could be cooked and prepared.

If a woman with a toddler needed to leave her child to go into the woods to gather fruit and nuts, she could ask a teenage member of the group, or an older adult, to look after her child. The development of language helped humans negotiate and come to an agreement on these social roles. To leave your child with another human also meant that you would have to have similar values and be able to trust one another. The person looking after the child would ensure that the baby was safe until the mother returned. In return, the woman would share her food with the 'nanny'.

This scenario is a very early form of 'paid' work, but it is far from organized. It's not clear exactly when organized work began to take shape in human society.

Organized work and slavery

The concept of organized and supervised work is intertwined with a history of slavery. For most of our history as a species, freedom belonged to a privileged few. The vast majority of people, in the vast majority of our time on the planet, were not free to pursue higher forms of work and education. Engaging in creative or scientific pursuit was only really possible for 'free men'. I'm sure that Plato, Aristotle and Socrates, for example, would not have been able to develop their thoughts, and gain the recognition that they did, had they been slaves.

In medieval England's feudal system, there were serfs and villeins: not technically slaves but they might as well have been. They were treated like criminals (which explains where the term 'villain' comes from). Serfs worked on farms that were owned by landowners. They had to pay a punishingly high amount of compensation for being able to work on the farms. Think of it as very high taxes, in today's terms. They barely had anything left for themselves. Moreover, serfs, just like slaves, didn't have an opportunity to gain a proper education. For most of human history, the right to education was reserved for the social elite.

Things eventually changed, and the situation for the masses improved, thanks to several important events. One of those events was the formation of towns, which made it possible for some villagers to move away from the tyranny of their landowners, to try to find other means of living. In Europe, the Black Death also contributed to driving people away from villages and into towns. Then there was the invention of the printing press in the 15th century, which made it cheaper and easier to spread knowledge – the internet of its time.

Quaker disruption

Another important event was the formation of Protestantism, and in particular, a specific sect of this religion called the Quakers.

Quakers were known for having an unwavering work ethic, and a spirit of entrepreneurship that puts the most hardworking entrepreneurs of our time to shame! So many of the industries that we know today and some of the biggest brands of our time have their roots in this religious group. Barclay's, Lloyds and Cadbury are just a few.[5] When I read the history of Quakers, descriptions of the founder of the movement reminds me of some of the disruptive entrepreneurs of our time. Here is a passage from *The History of Work*, describing George Fox, the founder of the Quaker movement:

> He was an extraordinary individual described by those who admired him as a genuinely good man; but he was a good man with attitude. His preaching was confrontational and disruptive…, disturbing the status quo. Fox was beaten up by one mob after another. He stood up and invited the blows with almost foolhardy courage.[6]

The above passage could just as well have been a description of Gary Vaynerchuk, Elon Musk, Steve Jobs and Philip Knight, the founder of Nike. Of course, not that they get physically beaten by the mob… but arguably, the equivalent of mob beatings can be seen in social media.

Another notable characteristic of Quakers was their incredible networking ability within their group. You can think of them as the influencers of their own time. The combination of their strong network and work ethic made them super-successful in creating industries that have lasted to this day. It's not surprising to find that they also triggered the start of the Industrial Revolution.

Revolution and the birth of modern jobs

We have many names for different kinds of change; some signify slight change, and some are much more severe. Some are for the better, and some are not, depending on whose perspective we look at it from. There are a few variations of change concerning technology, which is particularly crucial to the future of work. We call them: innovation, disruption and revolution. These three concepts often tend to appear in that order:

1 Humans create new products or services to make their lives a little easier – this is called innovation.
2 Sometimes, that innovation displaces some people – this is called disruption.
3 Disruption may then become much more consequential and impact a large number of people, at an accelerated rate – this is called revolution.

Throughout this book, those three variations of change will come up again and again. Specifically, in this section, we're going to take a closer look at the Industrial Revolution, which also had a humble beginning with a quest to make life a little easier. At the time, perhaps no one would have thought that it would lead to the sequence of events that would change the course of history.

The First Industrial Revolution

We mostly know the First Industrial Revolution, which was about moving from manpower to machine power, as the period between 1760 and 1830. But the seeds of this revolution were sown much earlier. One of the earliest instances of this goes all the way back to the 12th century: towns were starting to attract peasants who wanted to get away from the tyranny of their landlords. One of the earliest town jobs was washing clothes – a job done by hands and feet. The invention of the fulling mill, which used water-power to wash clothes, put some people out of their jobs. Workers tried to complain and slow down the development of this new technology – but no one listened.

Then, in the early 1700s, an unassuming ironsmith called Abraham Darby sought to create a cheaper cooking pot. In those days, most families could barely afford to have even one cooking pot, and Darby wanted to improve on the existing models to make cooking pots more accessible. Darby and his assistant, John Thomas, experimented behind closed doors. It was a highly clandestine experiment. When they eventually found out, Darby's rivals tried to steal his assistant. Some of them offered Thomas twice the salary, but he stayed loyal to Darby. Remember Quakers? Darby was a Quaker, with the same work ethic and passion. His honest quest for making a better cooking pot triggered an entirely new set of industries, which his children continued and refined.

The fulling mill of the 12th century was not enough to cause an industrial revolution. Darby's approach to ironwork was not a complete reinvention of an industry. Instead, he refined an *existing* process, which – alongside the other significant developments we've looked at – spiralled into the Industrial Revolution. (A more recent, and faster moving, example of this might be Steve Jobs' reimagining of how we store and listen to music, which led to the invention of the iPod.) It took a few hundred years after the initial experience of mechanization (the fulling mill) before the First Industrial Revolution finally took place. As we will see in Chapter 4 on the future of work, history repeats itself. Governments and corporations have often been notoriously slow in responding to this kind of challenge.

For a revolution to happen, the magnitude of change has to be much more significant and completely irreversible. Besides, an industrial revolution is often fuelled by change on so many levels, simultaneously. For example, Abraham Darby's discovery of how to manipulate iron coincided with the growth of chemical engineering and harnessing steam- and water-power. All of these events went hand in hand to create machines that could replace the workforce on a much larger scale, across many industries. That's what caused a revolution, even though it was a prolonged process, which took about seven decades.

The Second Industrial Revolution

If mechanization fuelled the First Industrial Revolution, mass production drove the Second Industrial Revolution. This revolution happened much faster than the first one, from the late 19th century to just before the First World War, and the concept of a 'job' was born sometime around this period.

> The Oxford Dictionary suggests that 'job' is a variation of 'gob', which means a pile of something and was most likely used by coal miners to refer to a lump or pile of coal.

In the early days, neither workers nor employers had an idea of how to communicate effectively. There was no such thing as a worker's rights, and no proper management system. People worked very long hours. Since there was no adequate timekeeping, some managers cheated and made people work for longer than they were supposed to. At times, the system was also abused by workers.

One of the biggest drivers of the early Industrial Revolution was the textile industry, which created a considerable number of jobs for almost all members of a family. Women and children as young as five years old worked in the mills doing the more delicate jobs of handling cotton threads. Men did harder manual work.

Thanks to the Industrial Revolution, people's standard of living started to improve. They got used to their new, slightly improved work conditions so quickly that when new technologies disrupted their jobs, they hated it. Some people fought to stop the development of these new technologies, and some even lost their lives.

Luddites

Have you ever heard of the term 'luddite'? They say someone is a luddite when he or she hates new technologies and doesn't want to adapt to them. The origin of the word goes back to an early 19th-century factory worker Ned Ludd of Nottingham, who became the poster child of resistance against industrialization. Ludd was an apprentice who broke his stocking frame with a hammer when he was criticized for working too slowly. From that day, many workers followed suit and started breaking machinery in factories. They used to send letters to factory owners in the name of 'General' Ludd.

Around this time the use of machines in textile factories was increasing. The factory owners were happy because it meant that they didn't need highly skilled workers; almost anybody could handle the new machines with minimum training. The hardworking and skilled factory workers weren't so happy, though! They were losing their jobs, and there was no one protecting them. In April 1812 a group of Luddites raided a factory in the middle of the night. As (bad) luck had it, the owner was prepared and awaited them with gunmen. One of the men, John Booth, was fatally wounded. When a priest tried to interrogate him, Booth said as he invited the priest to approach him, 'Can you keep a secret?' The priest said 'Yes'. Booth responded 'So can I!'

Famously, those were his last words.[7] The priest was hoping to gain information about the people behind the movement, but individuals like Booth gave their lives to protect the Luddite movement. Little did they know that the impact of technology was going to be much greater than any one person could stop. Ned Ludd was not the leader of the movement, but he became the face of it. Today we still use his name.

When digital single-lens reflex cameras (DSLRs) and smartphone cameras disrupted my industry as a filmmaker, I felt a little like Ned Ludd. I could see that a skill that I had worked so hard to learn was diminishing. My first instinct was to panic a little and think, 'Now everybody can make films, my skills won't be special anymore'. The art of filmmaking itself was getting diluted.

People relied so much on the automatic settings of their cameras that they no longer paid attention to the intricate things that added unique qualities to a film. This story of innovation and disruption repeats itself many times over throughout history: as we will see next, the digital revolution disrupted everything that came before it. Once again people and jobs were displaced, and many people felt like Ned Ludd had done.

From jobs to careers

Between the Second Industrial Revolution and the digital revolution of the 1990s, a lot happened – in particular, there were some interesting events which led to the creation of modern management systems and workplace cultures. We'll come back to some of those events later. For now, what we need to know is that during this period, employment became a fundamental aspect of people's lives. This was a time when jobs were starting to turn into careers – the main difference being that the latter made it possible for you to progress.

Knowledge work

One of the things that helped this new concept of a career take off was the introduction of knowledge workers. Historically, knowledge was not something that you got paid for: religious organizations, priests and monasteries were often the keyholders to the knowledge of their time. With the industrial age, that began to change.

In the early 20th century, as technology started to flourish, many governments put funds into research and development. Education became critical, and universities gained popularity. Many individuals from poorer backgrounds found that they could get themselves out of poverty through education, something that had not been accessible to their parents and grandparents. The structure of society was still hierarchical, but the kings and queens were less powerful, and the aristocracy didn't have a monopoly on all the opportunities. Many factory workers could see that their children could have a better life than they did, so they made all the sacrifices they could to put their kids through school.

RAGS TO RICHES AND HENRY FORD

One individual who played a significant role in all of this was Henry Ford. I have much to say about Ford, and he will come up again in the later chapters. He changed the course of history for the masses in so many ways, including by paying his workers above the usual rates that factory workers could expect at the time. Arguably, he had an ulterior motive for paying higher wages: namely, he wanted his workers to make enough money to buy his cars. For the first time in history, Ford made it possible for workers to have disposable income. With more money and more freedom, people started to dream. Not surprisingly, they wanted a better life for their children.

Ford became a hero for many young boys, who dreamed of becoming successful like him. Ford himself had a hero too – Thomas Edison, who had given him encouragement in his early development. In his youth, Ford had an opportunity to meet Edison and show him the plans for his combustion engine. He reminisced that Edison banged on the table and said 'Young man, there's the thing. You have it.'[8] Ford never forgot the sound of that bang on the table, and he later became a role model for many young men.

Some of the earliest motivational books about the stories of rags to riches go back to the 19th century. For example, Horatio Alger wrote many motivational novels for young boys with the theme of success and hard work. We can think of them as their version of Instagram stories with motivational quotes! In the 20th century, though, this type of thinking bloomed. Opportunities were still hard to find, but they were there if you looked for them. It was a very different world from what it was like for serfs, villeins and slaves.

Everything was going in the right direction until it was interrupted by two world wars in the space of the first half of the 20th century. The world wars were a setback for humanity, there's no doubt about it – even though they sped up the pace of progress in some areas of science and technology. However, the most significant cultural shift and change of mindset happened after the Second World War, in the second half of the 20th century.

Having just come out of the war, people wanted prosperity and a good life. Mass production led to mass consumption, which powered the economic wheel in the Western world, and middle-class society was born. It was the golden era of many things, including employment and advertising. Society could feel the pace of progress. Everyone, everywhere, started to think about how they could make their lives better, more comfortable and progress faster.

But things couldn't possibly stay that way. Remember the revolution cycle we looked at? Progress leads to innovation, and innovation can lead to disruption, which can spiral into a revolution. Human society was once again about to be disrupted; a new revolution was on its way. Once again, many people were about to be displaced, being made to feel like Ned Ludd.

The Third Industrial Revolution

Computers and digital technologies powered the Third Industrial Revolution. Although the first attempt at building a computer goes much further back, to 1837, it took more than a hundred years before the first computer was finally built, in 1941. The length of this period is critical. The pace of progress was much slower in the past. But as we get closer to modern times, it starts to speed up dramatically.

Although the introduction of digital technologies was a long process, two events pushed the digital revolution into full force: the introduction of personal computers, and access to the internet for the masses. As an older millennial, I still remember the sweet sound of the dial-up internet. Every time I connected to the internet, it was like opening a new window to the world. The term 'window' felt so apt for an internet browser!

The internet and personal computers impacted so many aspects of our lives, and the way we work. Many people lost their jobs, or the nature of their industries changed dramatically. One of the sectors that took an early hit was news reporting and the media industry. People didn't want to pay for professional journalism anymore, because they could access news easily and there was no shortage of opinion.

Over the past two decades, so many more industries have been affected. With the introduction of social media and online shopping, people's attitude to socializing and their shopping behaviour changed. High street brands and shopping malls started to struggle. Live streaming and new entertainment channels meant that people weren't willing to watch advertising anymore, so advertising agencies also took a hit.

In his book, *Vaporized: Solid strategies for success in a dematerialized world*, Robert Tercek argues that everything that can be digitized will be. When things become digitized, they don't require a material existence and physical space. They will exist in the cloud or the virtual world. Often, this means that they will be much cheaper, more readily accessible and commoditized. They may even completely lose their value.[9]

Digital technologies have had another significant impact on the job market. Today, most parts of the world – even developing countries – are connected. This has made it possible for many companies to ship a considerable amount of their work overseas to be done by cheap labour. In manufacturing, China has dominated the market with cheap labour for some time now. There are also large pools of talent in countries like India, Bangladesh and the Philippines.

Armies of online workers in developing countries are doing a massive amount of administrative, technical, and even creative work for Western companies. They can afford to charge much less for their work because the cost of living is much cheaper in their countries. Access to cheap overseas labour and the increasing power of technology have also led to more abundance in developed countries.

In his book *A Whole New Mind*, Daniel Pink points out three factors that have changed the face of the job market in recent years, which he has named as 'abundance, automation, and Asia'. Pink explains that we can think about the past 150 years as a three-act drama: Act I began with the Industrial Revolution and the factory workers who were defined by their 'physical strength and physical fortitude'. He calls Act II of this drama 'The Information Age', which was the golden age of knowledge workers – people who were analytical. This was a time when large corporations started to take shape and turn the wheel of the economy. Finally, in Act III of this drama, we enter the conceptual age, which defines the qualities of the works of the future that we'll cover in the coming chapters.[10]

However, before we get to the future of work, we first need to gain a better understanding of the three dominant work cultures of our time. These are the corporate culture, the startup culture and the influencer culture, which I will cover next.

Endnotes

1   Ferriss, T (2012) *The 4-Hour Workweek: Escape 9–5, live anywhere, and join the new rich*, Harmony Books, New York
2   Donkin, R (2010) *The History of Work*, Palgrave Macmillan, Basingstoke
3   Harari, Y N (2019) *Sapiens*, iBook: Vintage, Part One, An Animal of No Significance, The Cost of Thinking
4   Harari, Y N (2019) *Sapiens*, iBook: Vintage, Part One, An Animal of No Significance, The Cost of Thinking
5   Donkin, R (2010) *The History of Work*, Palgrave Macmillan, Basingstoke. See, for example, p 53, where Donkin explains how Lloyds Bank offered an alternative to city banks. Throughout the book he notes other examples of how brands such as Cadbury and Barclays were born from the same movement

6   Donkin, R (2010) *The History of Work*, Palgrave Macmillan, Basingstoke. See, for example, p 50

7   Donkin, R (2010) *The History of Work*, Palgrave Macmillan, Basingstoke. See, for example, p 72–73

8   Donkin, R (2010) *The History of Work*, Palgrave Macmillan, Basingstoke. See, for example, p 162

9   Tercek, R (2015) *Vaporized: Solid strategies for success in a dematerialized world*, Lifetree Media, Vancouver, BC

10 Pink, D H (2012) *A Whole New Mind: Why right-brainers will rule the future*, Riverhead Books, New York

CHAPTER TWO

The modern career landscape

Just as a company's work culture comes from its values, so does a person's own culture. Companies develop cultures that are driven by their purpose; their 'why'. Every one of us also has an intrinsic culture, and this may or may not match the work culture that we choose. Many people don't know their psychological makeup well enough, which makes it hard for them to choose the right work culture for themselves.

In this chapter, we're going to take a closer look at the three dominant work cultures of our time: the corporate culture, the startup culture and the influencer culture. Understanding the difference between these three present cultures will help us get a better view of where the career landscape is going in the future. It will also help you decide which of these cultures resonates with you and your personality traits – we'll come back to this in Chapter 5.

Corporate culture

In the West, the corporate culture has its roots in Protestant values; in particular, the Quaker values that we talked about in the last chapter. Many of those values – and the processes that developed from them – spread to other countries around the world. Just two centuries ago, Britain had many colonies. By the 1920s, British colonies covered nearly a quarter of the planet, in terms of both land and population. Many Americans are also of British descent, and carry similar values and attitudes towards work.

Although the Industrial Revolution originated in Britain, America reaped many of its rewards for the following decades – and they still do today. American industrialists had a knack for taking ideas from others and implementing them better than their originators. They did this in textiles, and later in steel making. America discovered how to harness the power of large groups of people working alongside industrial machines to increase productivity. They were also the ones who developed the corporate culture. By the 20th century, organized work had become a massive aspect of many cultures around the world, as American business consultants travelled internationally to spread their methods.

Scientific management and dehumanizing time

All of this progress happened as American business owners found out that they could increase their profit if they produced more products at a lower price. The question was how to increase the productivity of their workers. In business, we call this scale. Employers had become obsessed with scaling up their companies, and started to experiment with ways to increase productivity in the factories. Through these experimentations, they developed something called the 'scientific management' theory.

This theory evolved and became the foundation of the corporate culture. (It was also much more than that – this mindset of increasing productivity spread to other areas of society, from politics and education to families and healthcare.) The theory of scientific management is not one single set of guidelines; rather, it's a combination of ideas and approaches that evolved over several decades. However, there was one concept that remained consistent in its core, which is still present to this day, even in the startup and influencer culture: the concept of quantifying human productivity against time. I call it 'dehumanizing time'. As you will see later in the book, 're-humanizing time' is going to become an essential aspect of work in the age of artificial intelligence (or AI). Ironically, dehumanizing time took off with the invention of the watch.

Before there was an official form of 'clocking', time management in factories was a lot harder. Both workers and employers sometimes cheated in timekeeping. The invention of the pocket watch made it possible for both parties to track time. In the beginning, pocket watches were very expensive, and not everyone could afford to have one. But like many other inventions, eventually they became cheaper and more accessible.

Some factory owners tried to ban workers from bringing a watch into the factory, but this couldn't possibly last for long. Eventually, enough people had watches in their pockets that both workers and employers became obsessed with timekeeping. Bosses wanted to get the most out of workers within work hours, and workers wanted to do only the work for which they were being paid.

But the balance was about to change: two individuals would alter the way we measured human productivity against time, in a way that became the foundation of the corporate culture. One of them was Henry Ford, whom we met in the last chapter; we will talk about him some more shortly. The second individual is less known to the general public, but his ideas have shaped so much of our work cultures to date. Let me introduce you to him.

Fredrick Taylor and efficiency

When I first read Robert Kanigel's *The One Best Way: Frederick Winslow Taylor and the enigma of efficiency*, my reaction wasn't great – I thought that Taylor, an engineer, had taken all the fun out of work! By definition, engineering is about designing and constructing machines, and it turns out that Taylor was adamant that humans could be programmed to work just like machines. Like many of the influential characters that we've encountered so far, he came from a Quaker background. When he was a young man, Taylor hoped to go to Harvard University, but his weak eyesight meant that he couldn't pursue that path. Instead, after four years of apprenticeship, he started working as a labourer at Philadelphia's Midvale Steel Company. The making of steel was a big business back then, and Taylor was at the right place at the right time.

Partly due to his talent and hard work, and partly thanks to his family's close relationship with the owners, Taylor was quickly promoted to a managerial role. He started to notice that some workers were taking their time and – in his eyes – not working hard enough. There was good reason for this: since they got paid for each finished piece, initially the labourers worked harder to earn more. But the employers didn't like to see them make too much, so they cut their rates. Understandably, the workers started to pace themselves, which slowed down the overall production levels. This irritated Taylor, as it didn't sit well with his Quaker values and his mechanical approach to management. He did everything in his power to improve the output levels, from firing slow workers to threatening to cut their wages.

Finally, Taylor found an engineering solution to a human problem. Rather than relying on one skilled worker to deliver a finished piece of product, he decided to attack the very thing that the men prided themselves on, their skills. With the owner's permission, Taylor set out to conduct a series of experiments in reshuffling the way people worked. He started to carefully observe the steps involved in the making of each piece and broke down the process into all its elements. Finally, he assigned the men to do only one part of the process each. By doing this, he managed to dismantle the work process into its components.

Taylor's revolutionary method changed the nature of work forever. With his task-based approach, he discovered that some of those tasks could be done by unskilled workers. They cost much less than skilled engineers; and in addition, the task-based approach also made it easier to measure how much time each task would take, so workers could no longer set their own pace. The stopwatch was there to measure their every move.

Initially, this approach to dismantling work was used only in managing physical labour. But as we will see later, it eventually affected knowledge workers as well.

Taylor discovered ways to improve steelwork and how to cut metal with precision without the need for skilled engineers. He patented his processes and went on to become a very wealthy man. But he rendered many highly skilled machinists unnecessary. Once again, some people walked home feeling like Ned Ludd had done. Taylor eventually started a management consultancy, to spread his theories of 'scientific management'. He became the first and undoubtedly one of the most influential management consultants of all time.

Taylorism vs Fordism

Henry Ford never officially endorsed or acknowledged Taylor. We don't know whether he ever studied Taylor's work and theories. Like Taylor, Ford was an engineer who found himself in a management position. The main difference was that Ford owned his car factory, whereas Taylor was a manager in someone else's factory. Ford had a similar approach to Taylor, in that he also dismantled work down to its individual components. He took it a step further, though: his most significant development was the introduction of the conveyor belt, which meant that workers no longer had to move from their spot. By getting people to stay still in their workstations as they performed simple, repetitive tasks, he dramatically improved output and cut down production time.

The combination of the conveyor belt and breaking down the work processes into smaller tasks made it possible to replace many of the skilled workers with non-skilled workers. Eventually, it even made it possible to automate some of the tasks, increasingly taking humans out of the equation. Humans were still needed, but far less than before. Before then, one person needed to learn all of the processes involved in the assembly line, which made them more engaged and gave them a sense of achievement. But with Ford's new approach, each person was in charge of only one or two small portions of the assembly line. They didn't have to be particularly skilled to do the job, which was now much simpler and arguably less exciting or engaging.

Still, those who were fortunate enough to have a job started to make more money, thanks to the improved processes. At the same time, Ford was able to bring down his cost of production and produce more vehicles. In 1909 Ford's Model-T cost $950; by 1916 he had managed to bring the price down to only $360. In the first year, the company made only 13,840 cars. In 1916 they produced 585,388 cars.[1] This was thanks to the division of labour into more straightforward tasks and to the conveyor belt. On the surface, this was all positive, as people were becoming more prosperous and many of the workers of Ford's factory could afford to buy his cars and move into bigger houses in the suburbs. People had more freedom to travel to nearby cities, now that they had a means of transportation. They had more money to buy things, consumerism was born and capitalism bloomed.

However, although people could now travel further distances, their lives had become more sedentary. At work, they sat still behind the conveyor belt. They sat still in their cars during the daily commute to work. And, at home, they sat again to read the evening paper – a form of entertainment that was eventually replaced by television and video games.

And the process of chunking and dividing tasks, with all of the effects it produced, was not limited to the factories where it started. Soon, it entered the office-based work environment and affected knowledge workers, too. The employers had learnt a new trick, and they were applying it wherever possible. If they could break down someone's work into smaller tasks, it meant that less-skilled workers could fulfil parts of the work. Result? They saved money!

For workers, this wasn't much fun. Jobs became less engaging or inspiring: as 'time' was dehumanized and work lost its character, people became less engaged with both. People were physically there, but they were daydreaming, and their mindfulness diminished. Workers lost context because they were no longer involved in all the processes. There was no sense of ownership, or a feeling that you were allowed to exercise much creativity. They didn't need to use their brains as much, so critical thinking declined. Finally, emotional intelligence became less relevant as many jobs involved repetitive tasks, with minimum interaction with the rest of their team. (Remember these skills, and their decline – they'll be important later, in Part Three.)

By separating people from each other and disconnecting them from their work, Ford and Taylor's approach to scientific management increased production levels. The satisfaction that people lost in exercising their human qualities, they obtained in buying lots of new things, from cars and houses to clothes and gadgets. This was the beginning of modern consumerism, which became the main driver of a capitalist society. The Quaker movement, which started from a place of honesty, work ethics and a real desire to improve people's lives, achieved so many of its goals. But it also created a new culture that perhaps its originators didn't intend.

Does this mean that we should stop innovating? No! It is possible to combine innovation and career fulfilment with humanity, and that's what this book is all about. But we can't improve something that we don't fully understand, which is why we have to dig deep. The corporate culture is the most established of today's work cultures, but it's not the only game in town.

Startup culture

The definition of a startup I'm using in this book may not be what you have in mind. For this book, when I talk about start-ups, I mean mainly companies that were formed after the 1960s and have somewhat different values and processes in comparison to long-established corporations. If the origins of the corporate culture were in the management of the factory floor, the roots of the startup culture were in the rise of knowledge workers.

Peter Drucker was another famous management consultant, who was born about half a century after Fredrick Taylor. He was the first person to use the term 'knowledge worker', in 1959. Drucker was a massive advocate of the theory of self-management. He believed that people did not need to be micromanaged, and that they needed to have the autonomy to figure out how they worked best among themselves. Drucker had observed this during the war, when work teams often worked perfectly well – even sometimes better – without supervisors. He believed that if humans could do this in wartime, there was no reason why they couldn't replicate the same results in times of peace. At the time, this was a revolutionary suggestion. Even Drucker himself considered it his most original contribution.[2]

The concept of self-management meant that people could become more engaged in their work and regain a sense of ownership – the opposite of the separated, rote, production line approach. However, many business owners and employers found it just too much for them to entertain. They thought it sounded like a good idea in theory, but just not for *their* business. Like every innovation, there are often people who resist it for a long time until it becomes widespread enough. Although Drucker's innovative ideas of self-management were not immediately taken up by corporations, they sowed the seed of rebellion in many modern-day entrepreneurs. Entrepreneurship became increasingly popular, and lots of small businesses started to spring up in the past few decades. However, many startup founders were in for a rude awakening.

In his book *The E-Myth Revisited*, Michael Gerber suggests that most people start a company because they are frustrated with their old job, but they don't necessarily know how to run a business. Most people who call themselves entrepreneurs are, in fact, merely practitioners.[3] For example, someone may be an excellent graphic designer, but this doesn't mean that they will be able to run a graphic design company successfully. Running a graphic design company is very different from being a graphic designer in a firm that provides you with the necessary structure so you can focus on your craft. This is something that most people who start a business don't realize. I didn't understand it myself when I started my business; I learnt it the hard way! Some people eventually learn how to create systems and processes to help them scale up, but many businesses fail.

In the past two decades, the internet and personal computers have had a significant impact on changing our work culture, and the startup culture that began in the 1960s has come to maturity. There are a couple of notable differences between the startup culture and corporate culture.

Hierarchical vs flat

Perhaps the most notable difference between the two cultures today is that the corporate culture tends to be a lot more hierarchical. Driven by Taylorism, the corporate culture is built to work like a machine, and one of the most critical aspects of building a machine is creating a hierarchy of processes that depend on each other, but never come into contact. One cog triggers the ones below and/or adjacent to it. That cog is itself triggered by the immediate cogs above it, but it will never come into contact with all the other cogs or the source of power.

In startup culture, although there is still a boss or the mind behind the brand, the hierarchy is much flatter. This is partly thanks to a movement started in the 1980s by a former MIT computer science professor called Michael Hammer. He talked about re-engineering the workforce, which aimed to remove many managerial roles in a company. Hammer believed that new digital technologies could streamline many processes that previously mid-level managers did, and that this could save the companies a lot of money.[4]

Although on the surface this sounded like a good idea, once again, a huge number of people lost their jobs. Many people who were laid off went on to start their own businesses, and, inspired by this new approach to management, they kept their company's structures lean. Over time, the lean structure of many startups gave them an edge over the heavy-bodied large corporations. Despite their great effort in 'delayering' their management system, it wasn't so easy for corporations to change their cultural DNA. There are a few factors that feed into this key cultural difference, factors that help break down hierarchy in a startup culture and help shore it up in corporate culture.

First: startup businesses are often founded by self-starter individuals who are more interested in focusing on innovation rather than managing people. At the same time, they usually start with insufficient funds and minimal staff, so they look for other self-starters who can operate without them. All of this diminishes the need for hierarchy.

Then we have the internet. In the past two decades, the internet and social media have amplified the flatness of the startup culture. Before the days of the internet, you wouldn't be able to send direct mail to the big boss of your company. If you were a junior worker who wanted to get a one-to-one meeting with the boss, you had to go through so many layers of hierarchy. Today, you can send a direct e-mail to a large company's founder, or even tweet at them. (You may risk losing your job for doing so, but you could technically do it!)

The internet also made it possible for people to see what everyone else in their company is doing and their lifestyle outside work. This can create camaraderie among a company's staff… but importantly, it also makes it harder for companies to engage overtly in favouritism. If you saw that your colleague was going on an expensive holiday, you might question whether they received a promotion that you missed. The internet has helped break down walls of hierarchy that used to create a strict divide between people in a company.

Many founders of huge startups are also very active on social media today, which makes them feel more accessible. For example, Mark Zuckerberg recently posted a picture of him with his wife and kids all wearing matching pyjamas. Elon Musk posted an image of a bee wearing a hat, saying 'this is my pet bee, Eric'. Virgin's Richard Branson regularly posts updates of him playing with his grandchildren. Gary Vaynerchuk shows his day-to-day life in his reality series Daily Vee. For leaders of corporate cultures, it's much harder to display this level of social media presence. I'm yet to see the directors of Barclays and JP Morgan in their pyjamas, or the CEO of BMW with his pet. Now, this isn't a value judgement – a flat culture isn't inherently better than a hierarchical one – instead, it's a question of which one you feel more comfortable with. Perhaps you don't care much for seeing your boss in their pyjamas!

Left-brained vs right-brained

In his book *A Whole New Mind*, Daniel Pink argues that the future belongs to the right-brainers. According to Pink, ever since the Industrial Revolution, our jobs have been designed and dominated by left-brainers. The left side of our brain is responsible for activities that are analytical, functional, technical, logical, and textual or literal. Left-brain thinking is also a lot more linear.[5] Now, although the scientific accuracy of the left-brain vs right-brain concept is disputed,[6] we can use the concept as a metaphor for the difference between analytical and creative and intuitive thinking.

The rise of digital technologies allowed many of the tasks that required left-brain thinking to be automated. So, we now need more right-brainers to enter the business landscape. This could potentially give startups an edge over long-established corporations. Their lean structure and lack of strict formality can make it easier for them to shift their culture and adapt to this new direction. Startups also tend to be more open to experimenting and even failing. In a series of interviews I did with marketing directors of large companies in 2018, several of them pointed out that their companies were not so open to experimenting with their social media campaigns. One interviewee pointed out that had they been a startup company, their bosses might have been more relaxed about testing and the possibility of failing.

I think digital marketing is a great example where we really see the difference between the left-brain thinking of the corporate culture and the right-brain thinking of the startup culture. I have repeatedly observed that large corporations get too obsessed with analysing minute details of their digital marketing too quickly. Startups tend to be more open to allowing enough time and to achieving a flow in longer term.

The 'right' side of our brain, then, is responsible for synthesis, rather than analysis. It is where we get our creativity and understand the context of a situation. The right brain is less concerned with the details and cares more about the big picture. It also cares more about design and aesthetics, rather than just functionality. The right brain is where your intuitive thinking comes from. Another word for intuition is gut feeling, which means that right-brain thinking is closely related to our emotions. Taylor would certainly not have approved of associating 'feelings and emotions' with the workplace.

The importance of emotional impact in the startup culture is the reason why the concept of design over functionality has become so important. If you compare Apple with Samsung, for example, Apple is the embodiment of design versus function. It doesn't sacrifice functionality, but it frequently gives you a feeling that design is front and centre. Apple wants to appeal to your emotions, and Steve Jobs was a great example of an intuitive thinker.

Many startups that have emerged in the past few decades demonstrate more leaning towards the right-brain characteristics. However, we are still far from entirely celebrating our right-brain abilities. Most of our educational systems are still rooted in Taylorism and the corporate culture, which put academic intelligence and technical skills ahead of emotional intelligence. Even the concept of the IQ test, which we will talk about in Chapter 7, owes its origins to this way of thinking about human intellect.

Right-brain qualities are less tangible and less quantifiable, which is why they have been dismissed in business in a traditional sense. Although startup companies have incorporated some aspects of right-brain thinking, they are still concerned with scaling up and improving their bottom line for their shareholders. Capitalism makes it hard to get away from the Taylorist approach to work.

The free agents

Not all startups are gigantic tech companies. A few variations of the startup culture have become increasingly common in the past few years, which can be described as free agents. In his book *Free Agent Nation*, Daniel Pink explains that there are three different forms of this new work culture: soloists, temps and micro-businesses.

Soloists are people who work on their own, like authors, designers, artists, photographers and other often creative workers. This group has always existed, and as we will see in the next section, many of them transition into celebrities and influencers. The second group are temps. These are people who have been pushed to engage in temporary work, not by choice, but out of necessity. They may have been laid off, or be struggling to find a full-time job. They are at risk of being exploited by organizations that need them for specific tasks, but don't offer the security and trade-off of a full-time role. Many people in this group work in the gig economy on websites like Fiverr, Upwork and People Per Hour. And finally, we have micro-business that employ fewer than five people. This is a massive part of the Western economy. In the United States, more than half of American companies fall into this category.[7]

All three of these groups of independent workers often have a 'key person of influence' who drives their business. In a book of the same title, Daniel Priestly explains how building a business around a 'key person of influence' can have a positive impact on its success.[8] This idea has become increasingly popular in the business community, as many small business owners and free agents are finding that old ways of marketing have become less effective in the digital era. This new phenomenon has led to an amalgamation of business and internet celebrity and created a whole new culture, which we can call influencer culture.

Influencer culture

So many young adults today dream of carving a career for themselves as social media influencers. It's important to address it, since there are a lot of misconceptions about this possible career path. We will look at all aspects: the good, the bad and the ugly.

I believe that there is a lot of potential for good in the influencer culture, but there are also pitfalls that we need to be aware of. Influencers are the celebrities of the internet era. Let's take a look at how this culture has developed into what it is today.

A history of celebrity

To understand today's influencer culture, we need to look at its parent, the celebrity culture. Professor Fred Inglis specializes in cultural studies at the University of Sheffield. He explains that before there was 'celebrity', we had a different way of describing people who were in the public eye and carried influence in society. We called them 'renowned'. The clerics, the jurists and the scholars were renowned. It's important to understand, though, that there is a difference between celebrity and renown. People were renowned for the *office or institution* that they represented.[9] Modern celebrity, on the other hand, is a much more *individualistic* notion.

But how did renown give its place to celebrity as we know it? Professor Inglis rightly sees the roots of modern celebrity in the Industrial Revolution, which made entertainment accessible to the masses. As people had more money to spend on commodities, entertainment became one of them. Entertainment was the vehicle that has carried celebrity throughout the past few centuries, which is why most researchers study its history in a quest to understand this culture.

However, there is an aspect of the celebrity culture that I feel is less explored; that is, its correlation with the modern concept of work. I would argue that the desire for fame and recognition was a direct response to the dehumanization of work in the industrial age. Let me explain what I mean: remember Fredrick Taylor? He was obsessed with increasing workplace efficiency. Since he succeeded in achieving this goal for his bosses at Midvale, other factories invited him to help them improve their productivity. One of those factories was Bethlehem Steel Works in Pennsylvania, where Taylor met an unassuming labourer called Henry Noll, who was extremely hardworking and never complained. Other workers hated the new strict regime that Taylor had introduced; some quit, and Taylor fired a dozen others. But Henry Noll was an exception. He turned up every morning and worked at record time.

Noll became Taylor's favourite worker, but not as a person. Taylor didn't care about Henry Noll's personality or empathize with him in any way; he didn't even bother learning Noll's name. He called him 'Schmidt'. For Taylor, 'Schmidt' was 'an archetypal labourer, a unit of production that could be measured, regulated, systematized, and incentivized'.[10]

We also talked about how Ford dehumanized the assembly line. While Taylor wanted to make people *work* like machines, Ford took it a step further and aimed to *replace* them with machines. They both systematically tore apart the workers' sense of worth, one skill at a time. Over the years, their approach and practices became the norm in society, and most employers adopted their practices. That's how many workers lost their sense of individual identity. In this new economy, labourers were treated as replaceable pawns. It was good for capitalism and for *The Wealth of Nations*, as the Scottish economist Adam Smith puts it in his book of the same title.[11] But it was not so good for workers and their psychological wellbeing.

Now unable to find a sense of self-worth and individual identity in skilled work, people looked for other ways of making sense of who they were, and what it meant to live in this modern society. There was a tangible void in people's lives – and entertainment became one obvious answer to fill this void. Not only that, but entertainment reshaped and reprogrammed a new sense of identity in the masses. It showed them a world that was magical and mesmerizing, where beautiful women and handsome men had passionate love affairs and enjoyed a lifestyle to envy. In this dream, the lifestyle portrayed in the movies was the image of happiness. Most people didn't question whether happiness was really at the end of that line, even if they got there.

Over the coming decades, production houses started to put millions of dollars into entertainment – they released new movies at regular intervals throughout the year. Later, TV and radio joined the ranks, and modern show business slowly reprogrammed the masses from the ground up.

Celebrity and influence

Throughout the 18th and 19th centuries, celebrity became ingrained in modern culture. That's when the aristocracy, successful business owners, and politicians started to associate themselves with this new group of individuals. They understood that they could use the attention that celebrities won to sell products and even ideologies: attention became an arbitrage worth investing in.

People often think that the reason why celebrities are paid to endorse products is merely the attention that they attract. However, the psychology of advertising is a little more complicated than that. Remember that celebrity was the modern version of renown, and historically, this distinction was associated with high value, quality and respectability. People trusted the renowned individuals, and in the same way, they trusted the celebrities. So what made celebrity valuable wasn't just that they were able to attract attention, but that they carried trust. Politicians and people in business used their image to gain the audience's trust: that's what gave celebrities influence and made becoming famous so attractive. Of course, the money and the lifestyle were alluring, but the deeper psychology of this attraction was longing for influence and respect.

Arguably, the sense of individual worth that people lost in the workplace could still be seen in celebrities. Over time, celebrity turned into a more complex cultural phenomenon. People held stars in high esteem, because in them, they could see something that they didn't see in themselves – a strong sense of individual identity. At the same time, many people envied them and wanted to see them fall. As opposed to ordinary people, celebrities made a living doing what they loved, or at least it seemed that way. Unlike the vast majority of society, they were free to use their talent and express their creativity. This was a cause of respect and envy at the same time. It explains why so many publications were exclusively dedicated to celebrity gossip, reporting their every indiscretion.

The power of the screen

Throughout history, the renowned have often sought means to communicate, reinforce and spread their influence. They achieved this by printing their image on money or commissioning artists to paint their portraits. However, no invention amplified the power of celebrity like the motion picture, and the screen that symbolized it. Over the past century, we've been conditioned to associate the screen with fame.

As a filmmaker, I'm very familiar with this. I've worked with professional film and TV talent, as well as those who appear on camera out of necessity. Some people hate it, some love it, but one thing is for sure: *everybody* reacts to being on camera. They want to make sure that they look good and come across well. They sometimes ask to see the footage before it's published. Nearly every time we interview someone, even for an internal company video, their co-workers tease them. They say things like, 'Hey Dave, you're going to be famous!' Oprah Winfrey says that the most common question that guests on her show ask her at the end of each recording is, 'How did I do?'[12]

People's reaction to the screen fascinates me. Historically, only a small portion of the society, movie stars, used to appear on the silver screen. People had to make an effort and physically go to the cinema to see them. The advent of TV made it possible for more people to join the ranks. Artists, musicians, sports champions, and even newsreaders and quiz show hosts became famous. TV brought celebrity into people's living rooms and made it more accessible, but it was still difficult to become famous. The barrier to entry was not as high as it was for getting into Hollywood, but you still had to be chosen for your talent. Someone had to give you a chance. Today, personal computers and smartphones have made it possible for everyone to carry a screen in their pocket at all times. What's more, it's brought the barrier to entry much lower.

Meet the modern influencer

Before the internet, show business was exclusive to big production studios and publications that could afford to create and distribute content. Back then they didn't call it 'content', of course. It was movies, TV and radio shows, or magazine and newspaper articles. With the advent of the internet in the 1990s, ordinary people found out that they too could create and distribute content on the internet. At first, it was mostly in written format, as blogs and forums became popular. By the time we entered the 21st century, all the technological requirements were there for anyone with an internet connection to be able to create audio-visual content and post it online. The internet removed the gatekeepers of show business: you no longer had to wait for someone to give you a chance. Now everyone could have a voice.

Remember that for the past century we've been programmed to associate the screen with celebrities? Despite the ease of content production and distribution, people continued to associate the screen with fame, celebrity and influence. In the beginning, internet celebrities were not as big as those who appeared on national TV or in Hollywood movies, but they still managed to gain a degree of attention. For their followers, these individuals were a symbol of trust, quality and high value. That was enough for business owners to realize that just like traditional celebrities, they could also use the influence of these new stars to sell their products to the masses. Influencers were born.

Influencer culture: the good, the bad and the ugly

Now that we know the roots of the influencer culture, let's talk about whether this is a viable career path – as viable as a path in corporate culture or startup culture. One thing we know is that technically anyone can do it, although only a small fraction succeed! The internet and cheap production equipment have made it possible for anyone to be able to create and distribute content. So what else is there to know? Let's take a look at what's good, bad and ugly in this career path, and let's do so in reverse order so we can end this chapter on a positive note.

The ugly

The ugly part of the influencer culture is that many people pursue it for the wrong reasons. Since their intention comes from a negative place, their entire journey becomes a negative experience for them and sometimes for the people around them. Seeking internet fame just for the sake of it often leads to jealousy, constant comparison, and anxiety over people's reaction to your content.

If you think about the renowned scholars, artists and even modern celebrities who gained popularity for their talent, they almost without exception have one thing in common: they were pursuing what they loved. People respected them for their genuine passion and talent. Their fans supported them because these individuals brought them happiness, joy and inspiration with their art, sportsmanship or knowledge. Here's what we can learn from them: attention and notoriety must be a *by-product* of what you offer to your audiences, and not the actual object of desire.

Remember that the desire for fame and celebrity is the result of the systematic breakdown of individual identity in industrial society. Entertainment has been used to help us fill this gap by giving us a false sense of identity to make up for it. But as a society, we are beyond that now, and we can see right through it.

The bad

The bad part of the influencer culture has more to do with how social media platforms affect their content creators. All social channels' algorithms are optimized for one goal: to keep users engaged on that platform for as long as possible. Why? Because the longer users stay on the platform, the more likely they are to click on advertisements. Since this goal drives all social media interactions, influencers are pushed to their limit to churn out content at a rapid rate.

As a filmmaker and now an author, I'm active on LinkedIn. Sometimes, when it gets too much, I have to take a step back and remind myself that the ultimate winner of my efforts is the platform. I may or may not win clients, but it takes a tremendous amount of energy to create original content regularly. Social media platforms need people like us to create content and keep their users engaged. Remember that on most platforms, we don't get paid for our content. But in a way, we are working for them.

In addition to gaining revenue from advertising, platform owners benefit from something even more valuable thanks to our efforts. They gain data! Every time we post content and create engagement, their machine learning algorithms grow smarter. I truly believe that future platforms will need to be designed in a way to share the benefits of people's data with them. I will talk about this in the coming chapters, as we look at future opportunities.

Another downside of building your career based on social media is that you can't rely on just one channel. Over the past years, we've seen platforms rise and fall. Remember Myspace and Vine? Even Twitter and Facebook are losing their popularity. Snapchat had its moment in the sun but went down quickly as Instagram copied all its features. As of this writing, LinkedIn, Instagram, TikTok and Twitch are hot. YouTube is also still up there, but it keeps changing its algorithms.

If you decide to build an audience on more than one platform, you may be left utterly exhausted. Each platform has its own rules, content format, graphics and culture... which have a tendency to change all the time, so you may find yourself continually adapting and chasing new trends. Most importantly, you won't have enough time for deep thinking and inspiration to create truly original content. This is a huge problem for content creators. So what's the solution?

The good

The best definition of an 'influencer' I've ever heard is by Gary Vaynerchuk. Gary once said in an interview, 'An influencer is a person that brings disproportionate value to their community'. To me that's the closest definition to the concept of renown, which I feel the influencer culture should look up to. Today, one can be renowned for something unique and niche that appeals to a specific group of audiences who share a similar passion with us. It's much more satisfying to reach a smaller group of people and have the time and energy to connect with them properly, rather than try to be everything to everyone.

You have to identify your talent and know your audience, and then help them solve a problem or entertain them with your arts and creativity. We have an opportunity now that we never had before, but you can't let social media algorithms rule your life and induce anxiety. If you have something original and unique to say – your audience *will* find you. The biggest mistake you could make is to try to create popular content, as opposed to what you genuinely care about.

Once again, I'm going to quote Gary Vaynerchuk, who has a lot to say about this subject. I once heard him in a FaceTime interview with a young influencer from South Africa. The young man asked Gary for advice on what kind of content to create. Gary responded, 'I want you to create content that doesn't do well'! The young man was surprised and asked what Gary meant. Gary said that everybody is trying to create popular content, which is why everyone is starting to look and sound the same. To be unique and to stand out, you have to have the courage to talk about things that may not be on-trend. Eventually, your audience will find you.

Which culture do you feel suits you best? Each of these three cultures has its upsides and downsides. None of them is perfect. If we understand ourselves and know our own values, we will be able to find our place in the modern work culture. In Part Two of this book we will talk in more detail about how to know yourself and how to find your place in the world. However, we still have more work to do on our whistle-stop journey of exploring the trajectory of work. We've looked at the past and the present. In the next two chapters we will delve deeper into the future of work.

Endnotes

1   Donkin, R (2010) *The History of Work*, pp 146–47, Palgrave Macmillan, Basingstoke
2   Drucker, P F (2017) *Adventures of a Bystander*, Routledge, London
3   Gerber, M E (2007) *The E-Myth Revisited*, HarperCollins, London
4   Hammer, M and Stanton, S A (1995) *The Reengineering Revolution: The handbook*, HarperCollins, London
5   Pink, D H (2012) *A Whole New Mind: Why right-brainers will rule the future*, Riverhead Books, New York
6   Schmerling, R H (2017) Right Brain/Left Brain, Right? *Harvard Health Blog*, www.health.harvard.edu/blog/right-brainleft-brain-right-2017082512222 (archived at https://perma.cc/DXS7-LHBX)

7 Pink, D H (2002) *Free Agent Nation: The future of working for yourself*, Warner Books, New York

8 Priestly, D (2011) *Become a Key Person of Influence: 5 step sequence to becoming one of the most highly valued and highly paid people in your industry*, Ecademy Press, St Albans

9 Inglis, F (2010) *A Short History of Celebrity*, Princeton University Press, Princeton, NJ

10 Donkin, R (2010) *The History of Work*, p 142, Palgrave Macmillan, Basingstoke

11 Smith, A (1776/1910) *The Wealth of Nations*, vol 2, J M Dent, London

12 Nededog, J (2017) Oprah Says Every Guest Asks Her the Same Question After Their Interviews – but She Was Still Shocked When Beyoncé Asked It, *Insider*, www.insider.com/oprah-winfrey-question-every-guests-asks-after-interviews-beyonce-2017-9 (archived at https://perma.cc/NH3S-EAMR)

CHAPTER THREE

The future of work

AI and humanity

By now, we have gained a good understanding of both the history of work and the current career landscape, which gives us the context to start thinking about the future of work. As we will see in this chapter, context is critical. Our ability to understand the context of a situation is one of the crucial points that separates us from other animals and machines. It's a huge aspect of what we call 'general intelligence'.

AI and general intelligence

At the moment, only humans have general intelligence. There is no guarantee that machines won't one day develop it too; machines could, in theory, become even more intelligent than us, leading to an 'intelligence explosion' that would leave us behind. This idea was first introduced by statistician I J Good in 1965, and although it hasn't happened yet, we certainly can't get complacent.[1] In his book *Superintelligence*, Oxford University Professor Nick Bostrom warns about the pitfalls and challenges that the pursuit of artificial general intelligence (AGI) could cause to human society. AGI is human-level intelligence in non-biological machines. We don't know if, or when, this might occur: some computer scientists predict that it will be in our century, even within the next 20 years. We should perhaps take these estimates with a pinch of salt, however: Bostrom warns that 20 years is a 'sweet spot' for futurists, 'near enough to be attention-grabbing and relevant, yet far enough to make it possible to suppose that a string of breakthroughs, currently only vaguely imaginable, might by then have occurred'.[2]

So. The experts disagree... but what does it mean to our careers?

From the viewpoint of this book, there is no point in speculating about when AGI, or even superintelligence, might happen. The most prominent thinkers and scientists vastly disagree. Their views are also completely polarized on how the development of AI could affect the future of work.[3] Disagreements in predictions are so vast, in fact, that they fail to provide any useful recommendations for ordinary people like you and me. Some have given suggestions, but those are mainly to policymakers and top company executives. However, this is a book for individuals like you and me, trying to make sense of what all this means for us, and the good news is that despite the uncertainty, there are things we can do to prepare ourselves for the Fourth Industrial Revolution – the beginnings of which are already here.

What does this mean for me?

If the experts are all disagreeing, and we can't know for sure what's coming... then what can we possibly do to prepare? As with the idea of AGI, there is currently a lot of debate about how the future of work will look. Some of the questions being asked are:

- What percentage of jobs will be lost?
- Will the jobs lost be offset by new ones created by new technologies?
- Will governments pay people a universal basic income?
- Will governments subsidize services so that people won't need to earn much of an income?
- What will happen to the developing world, where governments are unlikely to support their people through potential job losses?
- Will AI create prosperity for all humans, or will we all be worse off in the end?

Spoiler alert: the answers to all of the above questions are inconclusive. As we know, current experts, scientists, economists, business leaders and politicians can't agree. Some, such as the economist Erik Brynjolfsson and AI researcher Pedro Domingos, are incredibly positive. They believe that AI could solve all our problems, creating a utopian society. Others, such as Professor Stephen Hawking, Nick Bostrom, Elon Musk and Bill Gates, warn against its potential downsides.

Some predict 40 to 50 per cent job losses.[4] Others suggest that we will see almost zero loss of jobs, as new technologies will create new jobs.[5] Other experts respond that not everyone will be able to adjust by learning new skills in time to enable them to gain further employment. Moreover, the cycle of losing one's job and having to find a new one is likely to speed up as we keep trying to adjust. Some experts argue that there is no real answer to the impact of automation, other than governments paying people a universal basic income (UBI), or providing heavily subsidized services. Historian Yuval Noah Harari points out a fundamental flaw in the concept: UBI doesn't clarify what is meant by universal, or basic. The US Government is unlikely to help the workers in Bangladesh, or India, for example. Millions of people in developing countries are currently providing cheap labour for Western companies. Many of their tasks are likely to be automated. Who will look after them? At the same time, it's not clear what is meant by 'basic'. What's basic for someone in England's Todmorden may not be basic for someone in California.[6]

There is no definitive way of saying who is right. The best plan of action, from where I stand, is to prepare. After all, our work has become a huge part of our identity; it's much more than about subsistence. Harari gave a good analogy in an interview, saying, 'If traditionally people built identities like stone houses with very deep foundations, now it makes more sense to build identities like tents that you can fold and move elsewhere. Because we don't know where you will have to move, but you will have to move.'[7] While that's a good analogy, it could have massive implications for our mental and physical health: in Chapter 1, we looked briefly at why we work, beyond the basic necessity of earning money to live. This is no small matter. Byron Rees, who has interviewed some of the top researchers and industry leaders in the field of artificial intelligence and written on this topic extensively, points out that even if we end up needing to work less, many of us will still choose to work additional hours to have a higher quality of life.[8] Most people don't *just* work to survive. In the modern world, we have grown accustomed to a certain quality of life. Many people would probably still choose to work beyond their basic income levels, even if money were handed to them.

Fear of the unknown

But this is, at the moment, a mostly theoretical question. We know there are problems with the UBI idea; the reality is that for the time being, most of us will still need to work a fair number of hours per week. But that doesn't necessarily make the career fear any less. In fact, it may make it worse – for many of us, the future of work is still a big question, and not merely a matter of intellectual debate. The mostly theoretical questions of whether or not artificial intelligence will overtake human intelligence feels less important than the very real question of whether or not artificial intelligence will render your job obsolete!

It's certainly true for me that these questions feel all too real. Having sifted through hundreds of books, articles and interviews on this topic, I feel underwhelmed with the same repeated arguments on both sides. None seems to offer a practical answer to what this means to ordinary people, and I know from experience that career fear can be very real.

HOW CAREER FEAR SPURRED ME ON

I remember my first real experience of career fear. I was working in TV and had been unhappy for a while. I knew that, soon, it would be time to move on. But I still needed the income and I hadn't been able to find a suitable alternative. Then one November morning in 2014, I was told in an all-too-brief phone call that a long-running show I was working on had been cancelled. I had already started working on the new season of the show, but just like that, with no previous warning, I was told that I wasn't getting paid for the work I had already done (but that I was welcome to pitch for a new show!). That was the last straw for me – I wasn't going back.

Despite the fact that I had been ready to leave, that didn't stop me going through months of depression and fear. It was a setback, and a very stressful one. Once I was out the other side of that stressful time, I promised myself that I would never allow myself to be taken off guard in that way again. From now on, I would take a much more proactive approach to my career.

When I talk about the impact of technology on the future of work, people are often quick to tell me that *their* job won't be affected. 'There is no way a machine could do my job', they say! However, despite the lack of solid answers so far, I urge you to keep an open mind and consider the possibility that change may come from unexpected sources. Breakthroughs in one field could affect a completely different industry. It's critical to be aware of both the challenges and the opportunities that may arise. For example, when British inventor Edwin Budding built the first ever lawnmower, he put some people out of a job. But he also opened up a whole new set of possibilities that never existed before.

Challenges and opportunities

Just like with the lawnmower, the threat to most jobs is not that we will lose them entirely but that around half of the tasks in many jobs could be automated.[9] One person at a London firm told me that instead of giving them a pay rise, their company is letting staff go home half an hour earlier. In the coming years, many people may find themselves having to share their job with others and work part-time, as machines will take over some of their tasks. Remember the task-based approach to jobs which was developed by people like Ford and Taylor? That very approach is now enabling employers to outsource many tasks that previously required human input to machines.

The good news is that history shows us that whenever there are challenges, there are also opportunities. This time, the challenges ahead of our generation are particularly difficult ones. As always, there are opportunities, but without understanding the depth of the situation, we can't identify them or prepare in time. Time is a big factor in all of this. The pace of technological advancements has been increasing exponentially since the advent of computers. Undoubtedly, computers are the most fascinating human invention, to date, and they are changing the way we live and work forever.

One thing is certain: in the next few years, the career landscape will look dramatically different. One of the key ways in which it *might* look different lies in the difference between emotional processing and logical processing.

Logic and emotions

Logic is the process of reasoning that aims to capture, systematize and formalize the validity of information.[10] It's important to understand that logic is not about proving that a statement is *true*. It can only tell you that it's *valid*. There is a difference between truth and validity: validity (and therefore logic) is concerned with the structure of an argument, rather than the truth of its substance. This is where we humans still have an advantage over computers, and it is this distinction that could make the difference between you having a fulfilling career in the coming years or not.

Here's an example: say you search Google for 'exotic food recipes'. Google's algorithm will do a logical computation, which brings up several suggestions. I just googled this myself, and the first option presented was 'Garlic Butter Baked Salmon In Foil'. Now is this *true*? Is 'Garlic Butter Baked Salmon In Foil' really an exotic food? If you asked Messrs Larry Page and Sergey Brin, they might agree that it's not exactly the most exotic food. They may not even agree with each other on how exotic they each find 'Garlic Butter Baked Salmon In Foil'. But they will be quick to remind you that it's a *valid* answer to your query!

This example makes the difference crystal clear. While Google might do an excellent job of providing you with logical and valid options in many cases, when it comes to a matter of taste and subjective experience like exotic recipes, you're likely to turn to food bloggers, or cookbook writers, or even people you know. You will consider their ethnic backgrounds, preferences and personal tastes. You will want to know if a blogger's taste buds are generally in agreement with yours. For example, I don't like sweetened meat, and therefore I'm not a big fan of Western BBQ sauces. To me, meat is supposed to be savoury, so if I'm creating a BBQ recipe, I will be asking people who share my taste.

The subjectivity of human experience is something that we can't currently explain. It's also not unique to humans: my two cats couldn't be more different! In short, subjective experience appears to be a property of organic life. The more complex organisms show a stronger sense of subjective experience. To the best of our scientific knowledge to date, it is impossible to reduce subjective experience to logic. Subjective experience is an emergent phenomenon, which means that it is far more complex than the sum of its parts.

Computers win at logic

Now, *truth* is (arguably) a subjective and relative concept. What's *true* for one person, a society, a historical era or even a species may not be true for another. *Logic*, on the other hand, is very different from the *truth*. While there is no such thing as a universal truth, logic is universal and therefore much more certain. Mathematicians, philosophers and scientists love logic because it helps them narrow down the information to its core structure, rather than to subjective experience, which makes it easier to process. Here is a famous example of a logical argument:

All men are mortal.
Socrates is a man.
Therefore Socrates is mortal.

Another way of putting it is:

IF all men are mortal, **AND** Socrates is a man, **THEN** Socrates is mortal.

That's how your computer thinks. That's the underlying logical computation that makes Google's algorithm suggest 'Garlic Butter Baked Salmon In Foil' as an exotic choice.

Logical arguments are not always that simple, though; they can get complicated very quickly. You build one premise on top of another, and before you know it, it can get tough to remember the previous ones. Throw in a few numbers and symbols, and your brain is fried trying to make sense of it all. Writing things down can help, but after a few layers of computation and logical processing, most human brains will hit their limit.

As we saw with all other technologies, we have always tried to outsource difficult tasks. Just as we outsourced part of our digestion to fire and used horses to carry heavy things, ever since logic was invented, humans have dreamed of a machine that could help us with computation. This was simply impossible until the past century because logical computation requires a huge amount of processing power.

Despite all this progress, the best that our machines can do, at the moment, are narrow tasks that don't require subjective experience. However, even without the presence of subjective experience, and consequently, the possibility of gaining emotional intelligence, AI can be a powerful force. It's up to us how we make it work for our society, or against us. To do so, we need to turn to another side of human abilities that logical processing can't explain or capture.

Emotional processing

Physicist Max Tegmark describes intelligence as the 'ability to achieve complex goals'.[11] Now, the question of goals will play a big role in how we look at the role of artificial intelligence in the future of humanity. The biggest challenge of AI is not whether it can be truly intelligent, and therefore whether it can achieve complex goals. By now, we have seen that AI can absolutely achieve complex goals – the computers are definitely winning at logical processing. In the words of Professor Tegmark, the true challenge of AI is threefold:[12]

1 making AI *learn* our goals;
2 making AI *adopt* our goals;
3 making AI *retain* our goals.

In order to answer these questions, we need to first clarify what our goal is. So, what is the goal of humanity?

This is not a philosophy book, so we can skip the hundreds of thousands of words that could be and have been written on this subject: for our purposes, all we need is a rough definition that fits our context. So, taking into account what we have already learnt about the subjective human experience, the best answer that I can think of is this: the goal of humanity is to *increase human happiness* and *decrease human suffering*.

Now, to a computer, that is possibly *the* most complex goal we could have defined, because it is a subjective and entirely conceptual notion. It cannot be reduced to logic; instead, it is rooted in humans' experience of emotions. Most human activities cannot be explained by, or reduced to, logic alone; rather, we are driven by our emotional quest for maximizing happiness and minimizing suffering.

Think about sports, for example. According to the Oxford Dictionary, the word 'sport' comes from the word *disport*. It originates from the Latin *'dis'*, meaning 'away', and the French *'portare'*, meaning 'carry'. It was used in as much the same way as 'to take someone out of themselves', and it originally referred to any form of entertainment, before it applied to physical sports.[13]

You can still say that 'to take someone out of themselves' is really what sport is about. When two people compete, they are both achieving complex goals. But they are not doing the act of sport in order to achieve a complex goal; instead, they are doing it to be 'taken out of themselves'. We compete in sport for an emotional reason, not for a logical one. We do it to make ourselves and our fans or our countries happy; to feel fulfilment or a sense of achievement and challenge. The experience of sports finds meaning through a shared experience of emotions. That's why we call it sportsmanship: it's about mutual respect for your opponent because whether you win or lose, you know how it feels to be in the other person's shoes. (This ability to put yourself in the other person's shoes is called empathy, or emotional intelligence, which we will talk about in Part Three.)

AI may be able to win a chess game. But without emotions, it cannot enjoy it, nor can it understand how its opponent feels. When Russian chess grandmaster Garry Kasparov famously lost the game to Deep Blue, he was able to take solace in knowing that at least the computer couldn't enjoy its victory. The *emotional experience* of competing towards a complex goal was not mutual. The machine could not experience 'being taken out of itself'. This would have equally affected Kasparov's experience, knowing that his opponent could not feel the emotion of winning or losing.

The golden age of work

So, what does all this have to do with the future of work? Some AI optimists suggest that with AI taking over our chores, we can all look forward to living a dream life. For example, Marina Gorbis, the author of *The Nature of the Future*, suggests many ways in which we can all find fulfilment by rising above the current concept of jobs, and money, and find new ways of making an impact on the world. I find all of these suggestions premature. From where I stand, there are many challenges ahead before we can achieve a jobless society. At least for the next few decades, I don't see the need for working for a living going away.

Instead, I suggest that we look for the answer to the future of work in our human capacity for emotion, by focusing on increasing human happiness and decreasing human suffering. Today we are facing a problem that can't be solved by merely reducing it to its elements. It requires a holistic reimagining of life and work, one that allows us to integrate machines into our lives but keeps us human.

Artificial intelligence can be our biggest ally in helping us solve many technical problems that we face today. Most of the global problems, from climate change to world hunger, poverty, ageing and disease, are all technical problems. We have the complex goals of solving these problems. The challenge is to make sure that we can harness the power of AI to ensure that it will:

1 learn our goals;
2 adopt our goals;
3 retain our goals.

This means that we all need to gain both technical knowhow and a higher level of emotional awareness, to be fully present and attentive to ensure that these alignments between our technologies and our complex goals take place.

Managed versus engaged

According to the Oxford Dictionary, the term 'management' originates from 'handling horses'. The literal meaning of the word 'to manage' is 'to manipulate'. Such was the origins of Taylor's grand theory of scientific management. That era has now come to an end. Humans are not horses to be 'handled' and 'manipulated'. I propose that we are about to enter the golden age of work, where we have the opportunity to create truly fulfilling careers, in which we are engaged and present, not dreaming of Friday afternoon and happy for each day to come to an end.

Times are changing. Many companies are starting to realize that connectivity and new technologies are making it impossible for them to continue with the outdated methods of scientific management. When the likes of Taylor and Ford came up with rigid ways of managing people in factories, their ideas were revolutionary and perhaps what was needed at the time.

In those days, ordinary people didn't have much choice other than to give in to the will of their employers. It was much more difficult for the masses to gain an education. Today – although there are certainly still problems and barriers for many – access to education is not nearly as rare as it was then. With internet access and just a little money, you can access any course and learning material, in almost any field, from almost anywhere in the world. Now, in the next chapter, we will explore three dominant categories of work in the coming years.

Endnotes

1   Good, I J and Virginia Polytechnic (2005) *Speculations Concerning the First Ultraintelligent Machine*, Dept of Statistics, Virginia Polytechnic Institute and State University, Blacksburg, VA

2   Bostrom, N (2017) *Superintelligence: Paths, dangers, strategies*, p 4, Oxford University Press, Oxford

3   For example, Nick Bostrom, Max Tegmark and Stephen Hawking have warned against the dangers of AI, while machine learning researcher Pedro Domingos, and Google co-founders Sergey Brin and Larry Page, are among AI optimists

4   Reisinger, D (2019) AI Expert Says Automation Could Replace 40% of Jobs in 15 Years, *Fortune*, 10 January, fortune.com/2019/01/10/automation-replace-jobs/ (archived at https://perma.cc/4ZHT-2WGE)

5   Heater, B (2017) Technology Is Killing Jobs, and Only Technology Can Save Them, *TechCrunch*, 26 March, techcrunch.com/2017/03/26/technology-is-killing-jobs-and-only-technology-can-save-them/ (archived at https://perma. cc/7DKM-JTB4). See, for example, comments by Chief of Staff of Redwood Software

6   Harari, Y N (2018) *21 Lessons for the 21st Century*, Jonathan Cape, London

7   Yuval Noah Harari: 21 Lessons for the 21st Century @ Talks at Google (Transcript) – The Singju Post, *The Singju Post*, 18 January 2019, singjupost. com/yuval-noah-harari-21-lessons-for-the-21st-century-talks-at-google-transcript/ (archived at https://perma.cc/94V6-MZKP)

8   Reese, B (2019) *Fourth Age: Smart robots, conscious computers, and the future of humanity*, Simon & Schuster, New York

9   Chui, M, Manyika, J and Miremadi, M (2016) Where Machines Could Replace Humans – and Where They Can't (Yet), *McKinsey Quarterly*, www.mckinsey.com/business-functions/mckinsey-digital/our-insights/where-machines-could-replace-humans-and-where-they-cant-yet (archived at https://perma.cc/ADM6-WAUP)

10 Almost every book that I've read about technological disruptions, artificial intelligence or the future of work includes a section on the history of AI. For the purposes of this book, I've kept it brief and only touched on the most relevant points to careers, but if this interests you, then one of the best accounts that I've found was in Professor Patrick Grim's 12-hour course, 'Philosophy of Mind: Brains, consciousness, and thinking machines'. This section includes brief points about the history of AI, which I have based mostly on this course. Of course, there is a lot more to the history of AI and computing than I give in this chapter. These are just some of most relevant points to careers and the future of work. Grim, P (2019) *Philosophy of Mind: Brains, Consciousness, and Thinking Machines, The Great Courses,* www.thegreatcourses.com/courses/philosophy-of-mind-brains-consciousness-and-thinking-machines.html (archived at https://perma.cc/D5HW-G2AR)

11 Tegmark, M (2018) *Life 3.0: Being human in the age of artificial intelligence,* p 50, Penguin Books London

12 Tegmark, M (2018) *Life 3.0: Being human in the age of artificial intelligence,* p 260, Penguin Books, London

13 Cresswell, J (2010) *Oxford Dictionary of Word Origins,* p 417, Oxford University Press, New York

CHAPTER FOUR

The future of work

Time, transition and machines

When I talk about the future of work, people often ask me what kind of jobs will be hot in the future. It's a tough question, especially to give specific job titles, since technology is changing so fast. There is no doubt that technology-related work is going to be in demand. However, in this chapter, I want to emphasize the importance of human aspects of work in what we traditionally think of as technical. In the age of artificial intelligence, highly technical jobs such as engineering, analytics and information technology have philosophical, ethical and psychological implications that may not have surfaced in the past – and as we explored in the last chapter, this is the key difference between humans and machines.

So how should we think about the jobs of the future?

Instead of specific job titles, I suggest that we think about our roles in society. I've done a lot of investigation into the kind of opportunities and challenges that we are facing in the coming years, and in my thinking, I've found three distinct categories of work that we will need in the near future. Each requires both technical and human skills. Each also leads to many subcategories and, eventually, you may gravitate towards some more than others. We can't simply think about these as tasks to be completed – these are *roles* to be *fulfilled*. The good news is this means they can't be mechanized and automated; however, they will require more effort and a holistic approach.

The three categories that I'm talking about are *time*, *transition* and *machines*. Let's take a closer look at each of them.

Reimagining time

How we think about our 'work-time' is changing. Automation is the name of the game everywhere, and as an increasing number of tasks get automated, companies will have two options. Either they will have to reduce their employee work hours, or they will need to create new roles where humans can bring value to the company.

In both cases, specialist roles will be needed to help companies redefine time and productivity. We will need individuals whose roles are to reimagine the value of human time. You can call them 'chief time officers', or 'time re-visualizers', or whatever floats your boat. If you are a free agent, you can find your own creative title.

These new roles will require a good understanding of human psychology, creativity, and a strong sense of emotional intelligence to be able to communicate effectively with teams and stakeholders. They also need a good grasp of the economy and the marketplace, and logical and analytical skills such as statistics and probability.

In their book *Human + Machine*, Paul Daugherty and James Wilson talk about re-humanizing time as a 'fusion skill' that companies will need to hire for.[1] The way that we currently think about our time at work goes back to the Industrial Revolution. If you remember, we talked about how Taylor was able to measure workers' productivity by breaking down their jobs into smaller tasks. He then used a stopwatch to time how long it took them to perform a task and set a standard based on what the most capable workers were able to achieve.

In reality, not everyone works at the same speed. Some people can work faster and maintain accuracy, while some need more time, but they may make up for their lack of pace in other areas. Taylor's approach to time management forced everyone to achieve faster results, but it wasn't so good for the employees' mental health. As if being compared to their peers was not enough, once the use of machines became commonplace, humans were forced to keep up with machine time. Now that automation is growing more widespread, it's become clear that we can't continue to measure human input based on machine performance. Nor can we measure all humans' capabilities with the same yardstick. So, practically speaking, what might reimagining time mean?

Individuals who specialize in helping companies reimagine time will be able to identify tasks that can be automated. They will also be able to identify new areas where humans can bring more value, through innovation and better customer care. These individuals or enterprises must also be able to work closely with transition architects, which we will talk about next, to determine realistic timeframes for AI transformation in companies. However, the truth is that most companies are designed to maximize profit for their shareholders by cutting costs and increasing profit. At the moment, humans represent the highest cost for most companies, and machines often represent increased profit. Computers don't get ill or need maternity and paternity leave. They don't get tired and don't require food or rest, either.

Reimagining time, then, will play an essential role in protecting human employees. It ensures that they are empowered to bring value to their work environment. It will also ensure that in the long run, the company will be better off, stronger, and more resilient against the increasing pace of digital transformation.

The idea of reimagining time doesn't just apply to companies. Entrepreneurs, influencers and freelance workers will also need to incorporate this new way of thinking into their businesses and redefine the value of their time. With digital technologies and AI taking over many of our tasks, we will all need to continually reimagine business processes to bring more value to our clients. You can point me in the direction of almost any business, and I promise you that I can think of a dozen ways it can be disrupted. Once technology disrupts a business, it often means that the value of time in that line of work goes right down.

For example, if you're an interior designer, many of the processes in your work may be assisted by digital technologies and AI. You need to remember that if you can automate and digitize some of your work, so can everyone else. Therefore, someone else might offer their services at a lower price, on some freelance website. Another way your work may be disrupted is through virtual reality applications that allow people to visualize their living rooms, or office spaces, with new furniture and wallpapers. With all these disruptions, your customer base might expect to pay less for your services. Or they may feel that they can do it themselves.

So, you may have to redefine how you use your time to bring value to your clients. Re-defining time is going to become part of your role on top of what you already do. It will require creativity on your part, and excellent communication skills for you to keep your clients engaged, so that they see the unique qualities that you bring.

Let's look at another example. If you are a teacher and use artificial intelligence in some aspects of your work, you may be expected to redefine how you bring value to your students. If you don't do it, the school may designate someone to do this, and the results may not be in your favour. You may have to show that you offer the students something that the machines don't.

So perhaps you can start to think about aspects of education that you can improve for your students, as AI opens up some of your time.

In addition to the workplace, another area where reimagining time will become increasingly important is in the family and in our private lives. As new technologies in medicine and health-care enable us to live longer and stay more youthful, we also need to redefine how we think about ageing and our relation-ships. In fact, the social and cultural implications of these breakthroughs are enormous. Although many of us may look and feel healthier than our parents and grandparents at our age, our society is still obsessed with age. There is a worrying sense of a need to achieve success at an ever-younger age. Social media and pop culture induce a tremendous amount of anxiety and pressure in people by glorifying the success of young celebrities, influencers and entrepreneurs. Almost every time you hear a success story, it's accompanied by the person's age.

Whether you are an entrepreneur, an influencer, or work in a large enterprise, we all need to reimagine time; and new roles will be born as a result. However, despite the best efforts of both companies and individuals, not everyone may be able to adjust to these new ways of working. That's why we need a second group of individuals and enterprises that can help us achieve a smoother transition.

Transition architecture

The next few decades are going to see a constant flow of change and technological transformation, not just in companies but also in our governments, families and personal lives. We all need to adapt constantly. Change is painful. But where there is pain, there is an opportunity to alleviate it and make yourself useful.

For companies to stay relevant in the age of fast-moving technologies, their leaders need to be able to take the time to think, contextualize and dig deep into their intuition. They need to develop a robust theory of successful transition. I use the term transition architecture to emphasize that transition has some crucial aspects in common with architecture. Remember Yuval Noah Harari's analogy about our future identities? Rather than building houses, we need to think about making a tent. That same analogy applies to companies and their digital and AI transformation. It's another way of saying that we all need to be much more agile and flexible. Now, a house and a tent have a few essential things in common. They both have a base, columns, a living space and a roof, but they differ immensely in their architecture. If, in the past, work was like a 'house' and in the future it's like a 'tent', then the role of transition architecture is to help people redesign their 'tent'. This means that we need to develop robust theories of transition architecture, and frameworks to prepare for the turbulence of constant change, while staying flexible and adaptable.

At the moment, we don't have a strong model for transition architecture. Remember Ned Ludd? With every new transformation, many people, like him, were hurt. Many lost their jobs and weren't able to recover. Technological disruptions and the pain of transition have been a constant state of affairs in business, as far back as the 12th century, when fulling mills put people out of a job. When looking back at the history of technological advancement, it all seems like an upward journey, in general terms. For us, living in the 21st century, washing clothes in the river with hands and feet is unthinkable. The technological advancements of the past centuries have given us washing machines, dishwashers, smartphones and TVs. On the whole, humanity has been far better off. That doesn't diminish the distress caused to people who lost their livelihood thanks to a new invention in the 12th century, and all the others who have suffered the same fate since then.

Are we superior to those people in any way? I don't think so. They were humans just like us, and they also had hopes and dreams, just like the people whose jobs are disrupted today have.

I'm often amazed when I read books and articles about how new technologies will make the lives of future generations better. That's great, but we also need to protect the people who live now, by creating transition architecture that takes human emotions and wellbeing into account.

When we look back at the past few centuries, we see a pattern of technological innovations and disruptions that repeats itself. The pattern is essentially the same, only its speed and magnitude have changed. We have enough data to learn from, in order to develop a sound theory of transition architecture.

Just as a house and a tent both provide you with protection, the first goal of transition architecture has to be to protect individuals. We now have all the knowledge, the technology and the ability to ensure transition doesn't hurt people. According to a McKinsey report, 'There is no doubt that significant change is coming. Automation changes the capabilities required to perform jobs, and it changes the nature of the work employees are currently executing. What results is more of a skills challenge than it is the challenge of a job.' McKinsey estimates that 'by 2030, 375 million workers globally and more than 30 per cent of the total workforce in the US will need to change jobs or upgrade their skills significantly. And businesses increasingly recognize that they'll need to take the lead in helping their people make the transition.'[2] Companies, therefore, need to bring in new talent to help them map out their transition.

Transition architecture for specific demographics

Transition architects could be particularly helpful for some specific demographics, including women and people of colour, for whom digital and AI transformation may be particularly difficult. An observation of the past few thousands of years of work shows that these groups have faced significant barriers to gaining equal income and recognition in the workplace. For example, a recent McKinsey report shows that women 'disproportionately carry the "double burden" of working for pay and working unpaid in the home in both mature and emerging economies'.[3] The report warns that women are potentially at a higher risk of facing disruption in their roles, since around 50 per cent of the tasks within the roles often occupied by women can be automated. Historically, women have had less time for personal and career development, since the burden of childbearing, and often childcare, falls on their shoulders. There is undoubtedly room for individuals and enterprises that specialize in women's challenges in an AI-driven economy.

We also need transition coaches, influencers, freelancers and counsellors who can help individuals and families to cope with the impact of technology as they go through transitions. For example, one of the side effects of the speed of technological advancements is increased intergenerational differences. These differences have always existed. However, technology has intensified their impact both in the workplace and at work.

In 2018 I released a documentary called 'The Millennial Disruption', where I interviewed several industry leaders about the impact of digital technologies on millennials. Now, millennials and Gen Z are both digital natives, but Gen Z is also growing up as AI natives. As a millennial myself, I can already see a massive gap between our generation and Gen Z. If the internet shaped our generation's behaviours, Gen Z will be increasingly impacted by AI. This will create a growing disparity in the experiences of individuals from different backgrounds and ages. Everywhere we look in society, we will need people who can help us better understand each other and cope with the impact of fast-paced technological transitions.

In short, with the constant speed of technological transformations, helping people prepare for and cope with its challenges can itself be a significant source of employment. This is not something that can be automated. It requires human input, emotional intelligence, a good understanding of the humanities, and technical skills such as statistics and probability to help you stay ahead of the transition.

Human–machine relations

Human–machine relations are likely to be one of the most challenging areas in human society for the coming decades. I left this one until last because it can create so many subcategories, and it can be a whole book by itself. I would go as far as saying that human–machine relations warrant a whole new discipline in our educational systems and in our workplaces. At first, I wanted to call this section 'Human–AI relations', but the truth is that AI is only one of the disruptive technologies that have empowered our machines. Machines have both disrupted and improved many aspects of our lives for centuries.

Today's technologies are increasingly empowered by machine learning, which I'm now suggesting will create a whole new set of work opportunities. The difference between machine learning and programming is significant for the future of work: here's an example.

With programming, humans give the machine exact instructions on to how to operate in a given situation. In this case, the machine simply operates in a deterministic way. With machine learning, the algorithms are designed to learn and find patterns in the data fed to them. Pedro Domingos puts it this way: 'People can write many programs that computers can't learn. But surprisingly computers can learn programs that people can't write.'[4] The implications of this are enormous; it opens up many new areas of work and study that weren't possible before.

Machine learning is arguably the pinnacle of computer science to date. Most of the automation that is currently deployed in many companies is still based on programming. We haven't even begun to feel the real impact of machine learning on a broad scale. As machine learning becomes more prevalent, the importance of human–machine relations will become of one of the hottest topics, not just in the workplace but also in our homes and personal lives. Companies are going to need human–machine relations experts on so many levels. Let's explore three examples.

Symbiotic training

Most of us working in the 21st century have got used to having an IT department and letting them take care of our computers. In the age of AI, the role of IT and other technical and engineering teams will be transformed. Technical experts will have to ensure that their team members have a good understanding of what it means to work with machines that can learn. Training a computer is not the same as training a human: we will need to prepare the humans so that they can train their machines. This is a whole new concept.

Until now, for the majority of workers, computers have been no more than a tool for simple tasks. If you think back to a hundred years ago when we used pen and paper and typewriters, our writing tools were 'dumb'. They were just mechanical devices. Early computers gave us an interface to communicate with our tools, but we could still rest assured that as long as we had our IT guys, they gave the machines instructions, so if anything went wrong they were responsible. All we had to do was send e-mails and perform simple tasks.

However, as we go into the age of machine learning, we are dealing with machines that not only take instructions from us but can also learn and respond. This means that we'll have to educate ourselves, and learn how to communicate with our machines. The magnitude of change is so significant, and it's taking place so fast, that we can no longer pass it off as something for the IT department. We will *all* need to become knowledgeable in the basics of AI and machine learning, and the implications of our interaction with machines that can learn from our every move.

Imagine you are the editor of this book working at a publishing house. Perhaps your company decides to introduce a machine-learning algorithm to do the first round of edits to each chapter that I write. This means that you won't have to waste too much time going through a huge amount of text several times. You will be set up with the machine-learning algorithm on your computer. It is your responsibility to 'train' the algorithm so it can learn to look for patterns of where you make changes.

Now, if there were a hundred other editors in your office, and you were all set up with the same algorithm, you would all be training the algorithm simultaneously. Depending on how you look at it, this is both the beauty of machine learning and the scary thing about it. It's like an intern on steroids – call it a super-intern! – who can learn from hundreds or thousands of people at the same time.

As the editor of this book, your role will change completely. You can now focus on higher-level work, but you also need to communicate with and correct your machine regularly. This means that you will need to have a positive relationship with your computer and treat it as you would an intern.

What's even more interesting is that you could learn from your computer too. Remember that the algorithm installed on your machine is also installed on hundreds of other machines. Depending on how they are set up, they are likely to be connected and learning from each other. Your algorithm may make suggestions that it has learnt from editors in other departments, and now it's transferring that knowledge to you. Now, imagine if your algorithm was also learning from editors in other countries, and other languages; perhaps it could learn metaphors and analogies from them, which it could transfer to you in the English language. This can open up a whole new set of fascinating possibilities for learning and creativity, as long as we are open to a symbiotic relationship with our machines.

Machine learning has the power to enrich our lives and careers. It's a question of how open we are to it and how we use it as an opportunity to adapt and grow. In a recent McKinsey survey of company executives, almost half of the respondents rated 'managing employee resistance to change and attracting talent' as their biggest challenges to adopting automation.[5] One of the reasons many people shy away from the technical aspects of computer science and AI is the breakdown of communication between technical and emotional skills. Companies now need technical people who are also very good at engaging their co-workers, to ensure that everyone can learn to work with AI agents as they would with humans.

In *Human + Machine*, Daugherty and Wilson call this 'reciprocal apprenticing', which is how 'AI like Amelia, or Microsoft's Cortana succeed in so many different contexts; future work will require a keen understanding of the dynamics inherent in human–machine apprenticeships'.[6] However, they also point out an important ethical implication, which brings us to the next point.

Ethics of AI

The ethics of AI is an incredibly complex area. One of the most commonly given examples of the ambiguity of the ethical implications of AI is in driverless cars. This scenario, or some variation of it, has been noted in many AI-related texts: you're in a driverless car on a quiet road. Out of the blue, a child jumps in front of your car. Should the car crash into a nearby tree and kill you but save the child? Or should it crash into the child to save your life? Who should decide this? The car company, the engineers, you, or your car itself?

In this example, there are opportunities for several industries to adapt to these new dilemmas: law, engineering and the entire transportation system. The way that we design our streets and our traffic systems may need to change; we probably need new laws and a different way of thinking about engineering. Lawyers, engineers and policymakers all need to face deeply philosophical questions that were never before present in our practical lives.

Had you been driving the car yourself, whatever decision you made at that moment was unlikely to have been rational and logical. Your decision would have been the result of your subjective experience and emotions at that moment. But if you are training a machine to make the right decision at that moment, the question of what's the right thing to do is much harder to answer. If the car decides to kill the child, this may not count as manslaughter. It could even be considered 'premeditated', because the car's algorithm would have prepared for such a scenario. But how can it be premeditated if the vehicle has no subjective experience, and therefore couldn't have intended to cause harm? The car will have to make a logical decision, but this scenario, like many others in life, is not a logical one. Until this scenario and many others like it are resolved, should we put a driverless car on the road?

Here's another example. When thinking about machine learning, Daugherty and Wilson point out that if machine apprenticing is implemented in a 'sneaky way', where employees don't explicitly know that some or all of their work is being used to train machines, 'both machines and management can generate distrust'.[7] Imagine the example of my editor, now having to work alongside algorithms. If my editor and her colleagues didn't know that their machines were set up with learning algorithms, that fact could create an unpleasant situation when they found out. They would be teaching an algorithm to take over a portion of their tasks, without being allowed to prepare and learn new skills to improve their prospects.

This is not merely something that could happen within a company. These technologies also have the potential to be abused by many corporations and even governments. Remember the interior designer that we talked about earlier? Imagine if she purchased software to digitize part of her work, but that the software was set up with a machine-learning algorithm that learnt from her and other interior designers. The processes learnt by the machine could then be automated and offered to the market as a cheaper alternative to her work. This could be a huge breach of trust, if the company didn't inform their customers that their work was being used to train the algorithm.

All of these examples are instances of where we will need to consider the ethics of AI. It's why companies will need to hire people to ensure that they meet people's rights, both as customers and as employees. Most importantly, companies will need to hire staff with a high level of emotional intelligence, critical thinking and contextual creativity in order to communicate these moves to their customers correctly.

And it's happening already: large corporations and tech startups such as Google, Facebook and Amazon are becoming more prosperous every day, thanks to the data that ordinary people like you and me create. Every time we create content and post on social media, or anywhere on the internet, we are training their machine-learning algorithms. Most people vaguely know that their data is benefiting social media platforms and search engines or recommendation engines of companies like Google, Netflix and Amazon. It's not until you get a good grasp of machine learning that you realize what this means, and the value of the data we are all creating for these companies.

However, the ethics of how our data is used to train algorithms leaves a lot of room for questioning. When we talk about data, most people only think about their contact details. But the real power of our data is in training their algorithms in our behaviours. In one sense, it's arguably a form of work that we are all performing, which is generating an income for those companies. There is a real lack of regulation in this area, which desperately needs a whole new pool of talent to enter the market and help companies address these issues.

Then we need to consider the ethics of how we treat the machines themselves. I'm not talking about the as-yet completely hypothetical scenario of AI gaining 'consciousness' or the capacity for subjective experience, but a more practical question of whether AI should have 'rights'. For example, in the case of the autonomous car, neither the manufacturer nor the driver may feel comfortable with programming the car as to whether it should save you or the child. You may leave that decision to AI. The car's algorithms could potentially go back through the history of all road incidents and find similar patterns. It could then extract what it 'thinks' should be the right course of action when the child jumps in front of it. Let's say the car decides to kill the child and save your life, but the child's family now wants to take legal action. Whom should they sue? Should they sue you, the car manufacturer, or the car itself?

If they have to sue the car itself, does it mean that the car has to have insurance, just as a human would? If the car can have its own insurance, should it also have an identity and other rights? Should we then change our laws about the identity of an insurance holder?

With the rise of the internet of things, everything from your refrigerator to your washing machine and doorbell are becoming intelligent. They are all, or will be, fitted with machine-learning algorithms, and will share information. Many questions similar to the ones above will come up. If you get food poisoning or have an allergic reaction to a substance because your fridge 'thought' it was giving you the right information, who or what is to blame? The manufacturer, you, or your fridge itself? So should your fridge have rights and insurance, too?

There are so many areas of ethics of AI that we have not even touched on yet. This truly is the topic of a whole other book; but it's becoming clear that there are many opportunities for new businesses and new talent to enter the market with solutions to these problems. In short, no matter what technical field you may choose for your work in the future, add to it a good understanding of ethics and the humanities. I promise that this will give you an edge over everyone else in your field.

AI psychology

Finally (for the scope of this book at least), another area where we are going to need expertise that did not exist before is in AI-related psychology. Just like the ethics of AI, AI psychology has huge implications in so many fields and situations. For example, there is the psychology of how a company's employees feel about working alongside AI agents; how customers feel about their enquiries being handled by AI agents; how companies use data about their customers to market to them; the specific psychology of using AI in education, childcare or elderly care. Be it in marketing and advertising or in human resources, AI psychology will have to be incorporated and integrated into almost every area.

Everything that we have learnt about human psychology to date has been based on an understanding of our organic selves and cultures. Over the past century, psychology has been an important discipline in business, management, marketing and education. It will continue to be as crucial in all of those fields, but we now have to add AI to the mix. It's no longer just about 'the self' and 'the environment', it's now also about 'the machines'. In the age of AI, we are no longer in a two-way dialogue with each other. In most situations, we are in a three-way conversation between each other and machines: they will always be there, listening, learning and impacting our choices. AI psychologists will explore how AI changes the dynamics of our lives, as customers, in the workplace and in the family and society.

Endnotes

1   Daugherty, P R and Wilson, H J (2018) *Human + Machine: Reimagining work in the age of AI*, Harvard Business Review Press, Boston, MA

2   Gómez, J, Hernández, P and Ocejo, R (2019) Four Success Factors for Workforce Automation, McKinsey & Company, www.mckinsey.com/business-functions/operations/our-insights/four-success-factors-for-workforce-automation (archived at https://perma.cc/QZQ4-NS3Q)

3   Madgavcar, A (2019) The Future of Women at Work: Transitions in the Age of Automation, McKinsey & Company, 9 October, www.mckinsey.com/featured-insights/gender-equality/the-future-of-women-at-work-transitions-in-the-age-of-automation (archived at https://perma.cc/5SND-ZUV4)

4   Domingos, P (2015) *The Master Algorithm: How the quest for the ultimate learning machine will remake our world*, p 33, Allen Lane, London

5 Gómez, J, Hernández, P and Ocejo, R (2019) Four Success Factors for Workforce Automation, McKinsey & Company, www.mckinsey.com/business-functions/operations/our-insights/four-success-factors-for-workforce-automation (archived at https://perma.cc/EUT2-Z3CE)

6 Daugherty, P R and Wilson, H J (2018) *Human + Machine: Reimagining work in the age of AI*, p 201, Harvard Business Review Press, Boston, MA

7 Daugherty, P R and Wilson, H J (2018) *Human + Machine: Reimagining work in the age of AI*, p 201, Harvard Business Review Press, Boston, MA

PART TWO

Mindset

In Part One, we focused on gaining perspective on the concept of work, and its past, present and future state. All of that knowledge is only useful if we put it into practice to shape our future. For that, we need to start with the right mindset. What's the right mindset for career success?

The goal of Part Two is to help you gain clarity on your definition of success, and put yourself in the right frame of mind to move towards it. That's what mindset is all about. So how do we gain clarity? By clearly defining career success and understanding our motivation for achieving it.

By the end of the next chapter, you will have a better understanding of yourself and will be able to define what success means to you. In Chapter 6, we will focus on some of the biggest challenges of our world today, so that we can use what we learnt about ourselves in Chapter 5 to decide where we can best fit in the world.

CHAPTER FIVE

Knowing yourself

As humans, we are changing in ways for which we have no previous paradigm. We can't go back in history and find a time when similar technologies comparably impacted society, and a few decades is a relatively short period in the study of a species. When Socrates said *'know thyself'* 2,500 years ago, he had no idea how crucial his recommendation was going to become 25 centuries later. So let's start with an overview of what we know about human behaviour so far.

In this chapter, we will focus on five main personality traits that shape most of our behaviours and how we feel in various situations. We will also take a brief look at three factors that motivate many of our actions and interactions with others. Let's start by addressing two different approaches to studying human personalities.

Personality type vs personality traits

You may have heard about personality tests that describe people in terms of personality types. One of the most popular personality tests is Myers–Briggs, which breaks down human personalities into 16 types. At the end of the half-hour test, you will get a four-letter code that claims to define your personality type. There are many others that work in similar ways, and it is very appealing to be told that there is a clear-cut answer to why you work the way you do – but the truth is that human personalities are so much more complicated than that! I'm simply not convinced that we can box people into a four-letter code based on a half-hour multiple-choice test.

Instead of personality types, psychologists now prefer to talk about personality traits: much of what we'll talk about in this chapter, for example, is inspired by a course by Professor Mark Leary at Duke University, containing the most digestible and concise explanation of personality traits I've come across in one place.[1] What's good about thinking of personality *traits* as opposed to personality *types* is that it leaves more room for change and improvement. Attempting to define your personality as a set 'type' feels much more rigid and less flexible; but when we think about personality traits as a spectrum, we realize that we have a lot more control over them.

Personality traits – OCEAN

Let's start by establishing what we mean by a personality trait. 'As psychologists use the term, personality involves those psychological characteristics that give people a distinct and somewhat stable and predictable style of responding to the world.'[2] Of course, we all behave differently in various situations. Someone who may generally be calm could lose their temper very quickly in a specific situation. But personality traits give us a reasonably reliable understanding of ourselves and other people.

I use an analogy in describing personality traits: as a film-maker, one of the things that we do in editing is a process called colour grading. This is where you use colour wheels to alter the exposure, saturation and colour tones in an image. When you mix these elements, you can create presets. You may know them as 'filters', like the ones you see on Instagram and your smart-phone's photo-editing application. I like to think about personality traits as colour wheels.

As defined by the Five-Factor Model (or FFM) developed by Robert R McCrae and Jüri Allik,[3] all individuals have five main personality traits.[4] These are:

• openness;
• conscientiousness;
• extroversion;
• agreeableness;
• neuroticism.

You can think of the acronym OCEAN to help you remember them. The way I see it, these are like the colour wheels in our photo-editing application: we can change their intensity and mix and match them to create endless possible shades of experience. In editing an image, we have five primary elements: saturation, luminosity, and the three primary colours of red, blue and green. I like to match these up with the five personality traits, in order to help me think about 'colour grading' my personality.

Now, would you prefer to create your own filter from scratch? Or will you accept presets installed in your brain by society, your family, circumstances, and your genes?

Nature vs nurture

The question of nature vs nurture has persisted throughout the ages, and scientists, philosophers and psychologists haven't always agreed. If you're not sure where you stand on the question, consider the following:

- Do you feel that you are personally responsible for all, or most, of your successes and failures in life?
- How much of your success or failure do you attribute to your genetic abilities and how much of it do you think is the result of your environment?
- Do you believe that you can override your genetic dispositions and environmental challenges?

How you answer these questions will significantly impact your decision making, actions and behaviours. If you don't feel that you have a high degree of control, you won't be motivated to take steps to improve them. At the same time, if you are not realistic about your genetic and environmental challenges, you may set yourself unrealistic goals that could leave you disillusioned.

Most of us have an existing theory of nature vs nurture even if we don't think about it. Most people are inclined towards one of the two following opposing worldviews, that people are generally:

A active beings who determine their own traits and abilities; or
B passive beings, moulded by either environmental or biological factors.

According to Professor Malcolm Watson of Brandeis University, if you chose A, you are in line with an organismic worldview, and if you chose B, you are in line with a more mechanistic worldview.[5]

The organismic worldview is generally more empowering; the passive nature of the mechanistic worldview leaves little room for improvement. If you think that your genes and environment determine your destiny, there is not much you can do to improve it. Conversely, if you believe that you can impact and shape your experiences, you are more empowered to do so.

BOUNCING BALLS   Nature and environment

Here is an analogy that may help you when considering your abilities and limitations and how they balance with the environment. Think of a tennis ball hitting hard ground; what does it do? It bounces right back up into the air. The harder you hit the tennis ball, the higher it flies upwards. When the ball is flexible and bouncy, and the ground is hard, you can expect an upward trajectory.

Now, the question is: what kind of ball are you, and what type of ground are you hitting? Are you bouncy and flexible like the tennis ball? And are you in the right environment to facilitate your upward trajectory?

What if you were a glass ball, fragile and breakable? What if you were a ball of steel, so rigid and heavy that you couldn't bounce? You could be a soft and squishy ball that chills and doesn't react much to the environment. None of those balls bounces high, because they are too fragile, too heavy or too soft.

Now think about the 'ground' that you hit. Are you hitting hard ground or soft ground? What if you hit the surface of a swamp or a glass window?

The bouncy ball and hard ground are often the perfect combination. But we don't always live in an ideal world. The fields will keep changing, and you won't always be the same kind of ball. Chances are, though, that by gaining knowledge of yourself and your environment, you can learn to bounce, and you will eventually find the right ground for you to thrive.

Let's look at the different personality traits in the OCEAN model. We'll cover them out of order – in order to look at the most important first.

Extroversion

Psychologists believe extroversion to be the most important of all the personality traits, since it affects the variability in human behaviour more than any other characteristic.[6] Going back to the analogy of the colour wheels, I like to think of extroversion as the degree of saturation. Like a highly saturated image, extroverted individuals (in the popular/common definition of the word) are louder and more visible. They stand out in most environments, although they may thrive more in some settings than others. People high in extroversion also tend to be more assertive, more sociable and enjoy being around people more. They enjoy talking and expressing themselves and may not much enjoy being on their own.

People often talk about extroversion as the polar opposite of introversion. But psychologists don't think of these personality traits in binary terms: instead, we can think about extroversion in terms of a continuum from low to high. Or, like on our colour wheel – a spectrum. This also applies to the other personality traits that we discuss here. Rather than trying to oppose them to their antonyms, think of them as a continuum. If you imagine the bell shape of the typical distribution of these traits in society, most people fall somewhere in the middle. As we get to both ends of the bell curve, you will see fewer people who are extremely high or extremely low in each personality trait.

Now let's look at the next most important personality trait, which is very different from extroversion.

Neuroticism

Neuroticism as a term has very negative connotations; although I've left the word in for the sake of the acronym, we can also think of this personality trait as emotional stability. If extroversion was like the saturation of an image, emotional stability would be the image's luminosity – how bright or dark an image is. This personality trait has to do with how often and how intensely someone experiences negative emotions, like anxiety, sadness, frustration, fear and anger. Because of the negative features of this personality trait, some researchers even call it negative emotionality. Just like an underexposed image, neuroticism can cast a darker shadow on our overall experiences.

People who are high in neuroticism tend to feel more insecure and vulnerable. They may be highly sensitive, and seem to overreact to typical day-to-day hassles and frustrations. They can lose their temper and get angry very quickly, and experience less satisfaction no matter how much their conditions improve. It's no surprise that people with high levels of neuroticism tend to have more difficulty with interpersonal relationships. Since a high level of stress can cause many health problems, they may also be less healthy.

Neuroticism has a strong genetic component, although environmental factors also play a significant role in forming this personality trait, especially during childhood. Does this mean that people who have a higher predisposition to neuroticism can't be happy and successful? Absolutely not! Remember, we have five main personality traits. We can mix them like we would on our colour wheel, pushing the bar higher on some characteristics to make up for where we may feel we are lacking.

Agreeableness

Agreeableness determines how positively you feel towards other people, and if you generally get along with people easily. This is different from extroversion; someone may be extroverted but not necessarily agreeable. Or they may be agreeable but not enjoy too much interaction. People who are low in agreeableness tend to come across as grumpy and not very nice to be around. On the other hand, highly agreeable people tend to be considerate, kind and helpful.

Fortunately, most of us fall somewhere in the middle. You don't want to be too agreeable; otherwise, just like a squishy ball, you could be easily influenced by others. People who are too agreeable find it harder to form their own opinions and may be too eager to please everyone. They also often feel more optimistic and have a more positive view of other people, which may sound good. But it could sometimes work to their disadvantage if they go too far. Highly agreeable people also try to avoid conflict. It is important to them that everyone gets along. They don't like to overpower others, or use force. They tend to be more interested in collaboration and don't enjoy having to compete. Having positive relationships is quite crucial to agreeable people, which is why they tend to accept people as they are. They also have more empathy with others and tend to be kind and understanding. They don't like to see others suffering and do what they can to help.

Agreeableness is one of those traits that's often shaped quite early on in childhood. By the time we reach adolescence, this personality trait will have taken shape in our behaviours. Overall, it's more helpful to be on the slightly higher end of agreeableness – but be careful that you don't get too easily influenced. If you are too agreeable you may find it hard to thrive in leadership positions, since you may not enjoy having to make tough decisions involving other people.

Conscientiousness

This trait is very interesting, because it can have different interpretations in different situations.

Generally, this trait has to do with how dependable and responsible people are. By definition, conscientious people tend to care about rules and regulations and do what they're supposed to do. They also tend to be orderly and organized, they are known to be hardworking and they try to do everything well when they take on responsibility. They probably have a high level of self-discipline, meaning that they can make themselves do what needs to be done, even if it may be hard.

What's interesting about this character trait is that someone could be highly conscientious in one area and yet show a lower level of conscientiousness in another environment. For example, someone may be highly responsible and dependable in their working environment, but at home, they may be rather untidy and disorganized. I'm one of those people: I've often struggled to keep my closets completely tidy, but when it comes to paying bills, looking after staff and film crew, and keeping promises to our clients, I fulfil my duties with a do-or-die attitude.

When it comes to self-discipline, you may find that you excel in some areas but flunk in others. For example, I've managed to develop some very good habits, such as meditating twice a day, exercising regularly and not drinking during the workweek – but there are some areas where I still struggle. For example, going to bed on time is never easy; and I often forget to eat during the day. And of course, we have already seen that I struggle with tidiness. If, like me, you are more conscientious in some areas than others, consider that some of your other personality traits or the motivations that we will talk about later in this chapter may be at play.

Openness

The kind of openness that we are talking about here is about intellectual and experiential openness – being open to new and different ideas and experiences. Being highly open makes you more imaginative. It also makes you more intellectually humble and less dogmatic. Openness makes you more flexible in adopting new ways of doing things, even if they go against your genetic dispositions or environmental boundaries and limitations.

People who are high in openness tend to be more innovative. At times they may even struggle to adapt to traditional environments, which could get them into trouble. Highly open people may also be rebellious and nonconformist at times. Open people are often the disruptors of their time, be it in business, science or technology.

Openness may seem like a clearly positive trait, but many people don't find it so desirable after all, once they learn more about it. If you are not sure where you stand in your level of openness, ask yourself the following questions:

- How important are traditional family, or national, values to you?
- How much do you value conventional experiences in life?
- If you were getting married, how important would it be for you to have a conventional wedding ceremony?
- How conventional are your views regarding the roles of men and women in society and in the family?
- How about your scientific worldview?
- How sure are you about your spiritual beliefs or lack thereof?
- How do you feel about the royal family?
- If you are a business owner, do you find the constant changes in consumer behaviour frustrating?
- Are you generally open to adopting new technologies, or do you get discouraged by having to change and upgrade your devices and software constantly?

Although the above are only some simple examples of openness in day-to-day life, they are likely to be good indicators over your overall level of openness. If traditions are important to you, and if you feel very strongly about your scientific or spiritual worldview, you may score lower in openness.

Similar to the trait of conscientiousness, people may vary significantly in their degree of openness in some areas, over others. For example, someone may be highly assured of their spiritual beliefs, and care about conventions and traditions, but they may be very open in business.

However, overall, you will know whether you are generally a more open person or not.

Now, so far in this chapter, we have talked about the five main personality traits. There are, however, three other significant factors that impact our decisions and behaviours. These are not personality traits, per se. But they are three underlying motives in many of our actions, so let's take a quick look at them.

WHAT'S YOUR PRESET?

Although I strongly believe it is unhelpful to categorize personalities by 'types', it can be helpful to look at these traits in a quantitative way, in order to better understand your starting point. Thinking back to the colour wheel analogy, this would be like your 'preset', or your custom filter.

Looking back at the descriptions of the five personality traits, where do you fall on the different scales? Mark yourself on the scales in Figure 5.1, where 10 is the most extreme version of that particular trait, and 0 is the most extreme *absence* of that particular trait.

What do you think? Where do you fall now? Has that changed over time? Do you have different scores in different traits for different areas of your life?

FIGURE 5.1   OCEAN scale

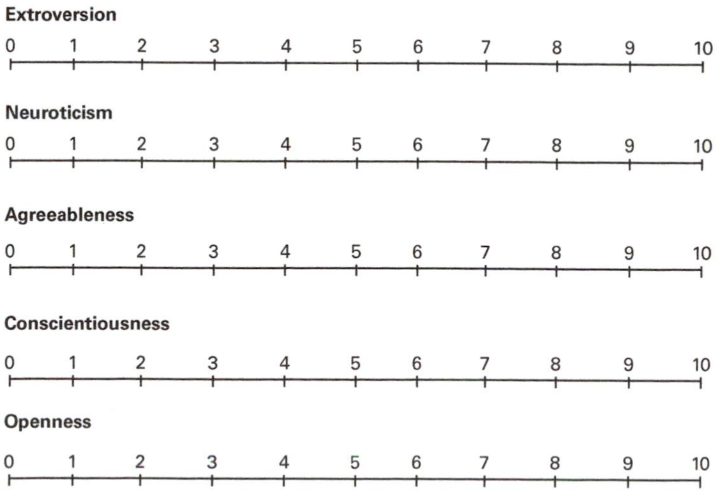

Extroversion

0   1   2   3   4   5   6   7   8   9   10

Neuroticism

0   1   2   3   4   5   6   7   8   9   10

Agreeableness

0   1   2   3   4   5   6   7   8   9   10

Conscientiousness

0   1   2   3   4   5   6   7   8   9   10

Openness

0   1   2   3   4   5   6   7   8   9   10

What motivates you?

In addition to our personality traits, there are three fundamental factors which motivate how we behave and interact with others. These motivators are:

- affiliation;
- power;
- achievement.

They determine how much we enjoy affiliating with other people, how much we try to have power and influence over them, and finally how motivated we are to achieve. If there is a mismatch between our motivation and our personality traits, we may feel frustrated and struggle to find the right environment to fit in. This is especially true if we are not aware of our motivations and personality traits.

For example, say someone is not high in extroversion but they are highly achievement oriented. Now if this person's career requires them to give a lot of public presentations, the achievement orientation may encourage them to push themselves beyond their comfort zone. This is likely to require a lot of deliberate effort and so the person has to be conscious of why they are choosing to go the extra mile.

Our personality traits and motivations aren't always in line. You have to dig deep to decide which ones are more important to you and your career success – which brings us neatly to the final part of this chapter, where we will discuss what success means to you.

What does success mean to you?

Most people mainly think about career success in terms of the following three dimensions:

- money;
- (positive) impact;
- recognition.

Try to answer the following questions as honestly as you can:

1 *How much money do you need to earn
to be happy, and WHY?*
This one is relatively simple. Beyond providing a certain level of comfort, more money doesn't always make people happier. But people often still pursue money even if they are 'comfortable' because they believe that those with higher levels of income are happier still.[7] So it's essential to know how much is enough for you and, more importantly, why that amount is your goal.

2 *How big a (positive) impact do you want to make?*
Not everyone is looking to make a positive impact. Some people see success in terms of impact, regardless of whether it's positive or negative: fortunately, though, most people are pursuing a positive impact, in line with the goal of increasing human happiness and decreasing human suffering. The question is: what degree of impact do *you* need to make you happy?

Another way to think about this question is: how many lives do you want to touch? Do you want to look after your family, impact your local community, improve the conditions of your city, or country? Or, do you want to make a global impact and touch millions of lives? Just as with the previous question, ask yourself why.

3 *How much recognition do you need to be happy?*
Sometimes people confuse impact with recognition. We must separate these two and clarify how important it is for us to be recognized for our contribution. For example, you may work as a junior member of a large organization, contributing to a significant global concern, such as climate change. But other than your close friends and family, no one else may know how important your work is.

Is it enough, if only you and your family know about your work? Or do you want to be recognized by everyone in your company, your town, your country, and globally? Likewise, if you were an artist, entrepreneur or author, is the size of recognition important to you? Why?

VERSIONS OF SUCCESS

Let's look at a hypothetical example. Ask yourself: which of the three dimensions of success do you value more?

Imagine you are a talented musician who has written great songs, but somehow you've never managed to break through. A few years later another band covers one of your songs, and all of a sudden it becomes a massive hit. Now, for generations, most people hearing the song may attribute it to the band that covered it. You may never get the recognition that you deserve, but your song has touched many lives.

In this example, you have made an impact, but you haven't gained the recognition or the money. Would you still be happy, and consider yourself successful?

What if you receive a considerable amount of money in royalties? You will have made an impact and earned money, but you still haven't got the fame and recognition. Would you be happy then?

One size does not fit all

Whatever your answer to the above questions, remember that there is no right or wrong way. Don't judge yourself if you answer honestly and get different answers from those you think you 'should' have. Don't share your answers with anyone else: your definition of success is not theirs to judge.

We will look at this more in Part Three, where we will also talk about statistics and probability and why you may want to come back and review your answers. So far, we have gained much deeper knowledge about ourselves and defined success for ourselves. We are now ready to find our place in the world, which is what the next chapter is all about.

Endnotes

1   Leary, M (2019) Human Personality Traits, Tests, and Types, The Great Courses Plus, www.thegreatcoursesplus.com/show/why_you_are_who_you_ are_investigations_into_human_personality (archived at https://perma.cc/SPM7-HPVV)

2   Leary, M (2019) Human Personality Traits, Tests, and Types, The Great Courses Plus, Part 1-Track 2, www.thegreatcoursesplus.com/show/why_you_are_who_ you_are_investigations_into_human_personality (archived at https://perma.cc/ SPM7-HPVV)

3   McCrae, R R and Allik, J (2002) *The Five-Factor Model of Personality Across Cultures*, Kluwer Academic/Plenum Publishers, New York

4   The Big Five theory was developed as a result of work and research by a number of psychologists over a few decades starting in the 1930s. Initially, psychologists Gordon Allport and Henry Odbert came up with 4,500 terms that they could find in Webster's *New International Dictionary* to describe personality traits. But, of course, most of those terms were variations of the same words. Robert McCrae and Paul Costa developed the Five-Factor Model which reduced all those variations to just five factors: extroversion, neuroticism, agreeableness, conscientiousness and openness

5   Watson, M W (2018) Theories of Human Development, The Great Courses Plus, www.thegreatcourses.com/courses/theories-of-human-development.html (archived at https://perma.cc/ULB5-N2MH)

6   Leary, M (2019) Human Personality Traits, Tests and Types, The Great Courses Plus, www.thegreatcoursesplus.com/show/why_you_are_who_you_are_ investigations_into_human_personality (archived at https://perma.cc/SPM7-HPVV)

7   See for example the study by Aknin, L B, Norton, M I and Dunn, E W (2009) From wealth to well-being? Money matters, but less than people think, *The Journal of Positive Psychology*, 4 (6), pp 523–27, doi: 10.1080/17439760903271421

CHAPTER SIX

Your place in the world

One of my earliest childhood memories is when my parents gave me a plastic globe for my birthday at age five. I didn't have any opportunities to travel internationally, growing up, and I was fascinated by how life on the rest of the planet could be different. My fascination with the world and the question of our place in it has stayed with me throughout my life. In this chapter, my goal is to help you find your place in the world.

We, humans, are social beings. Our lives find meaning in relation to the rest of the world, how we perceive our place in it and how the world perceives us.

Circles and defining otherness

We can think about our place in the world in terms of some inner and outer circles. It looks something like Figure 6.1

FIGURE 6.1 Circles of relationship

At the centre of the innermost circle, you will find yourself. At the widest and farthest point of the outer circle is our observable universe as defined by the laws of physics. You will notice that there is a point beyond which the term 'your' turns into 'our': the difference between those two words is only one letter, yet it's enough to define our differences, as well as our common purpose and meaning in life.

The concept of inner and outer circles is the source of how we define otherness. When children are born, they have no sense of where they end and the outside world begins. There are no inner or outer circles; everything is one. As they grow up, they develop a sense of self, and begin to define themselves within these circles.

Between you as a person and the universe at its farthest, you have your family, your city or town, your country, our species, our planet Earth, our solar system, our galaxy and our universe. The way we define our inner and outer circles determines how we find our place in the world. I always like to go as deep and as broad as possible, so I will start with our universe.

Our universe

When we think about our place in the universe, we have to start by going back to the Big Bang, to gain perspective and context at the most in-depth and broadest level. It's taken nearly 14 billion years of evolution for us humans to get to where we are today. When we look at it this way, we are both incredibly unique and utterly insignificant in the cosmic picture.

We are unique, because we may well be the only entities in the entire universe who possess the ability to think and reflect on their being and mortality. Now, homo sapiens has only been around for 28,000 years. In comparison to the whole universe and its history, we are like the tip of a pin. The first view makes me feel hugely responsible, to make sure I make something worthwhile of my life on Earth. The second view makes me feel incredibly humble when thinking about my place in the world and my personal goals in life. How does each perspective make you feel about yourself and your goals?

Where do our goals come from?

I've always been fascinated by the concept of goals. The kind of goal-oriented behaviour that humans display is very different from anything else we see in the world. Or is it? On the surface, people appear to have very different goals from, say, a ray of light. But when we break them down to their most nuclear level, our goals seem to have more in common with the rest of nature than we may be aware of.

Professor Max Tegmark explains that 'the ultimate route of goal-oriented behaviour can be found in the laws of physics themselves, and manifest themselves even in simple processes that don't involve life'.[1] He gives an example of a lifeguard running to rescue a swimmer on the beach, comparing the chosen trajectory to a ray of light: in the same way that we would expect the lifeguard to bend their path, because they can run faster on the beach than in the water, so Professor Tegmark points out that a ray of light will bend in a similar fashion, according to Fermat's Principle. Both the lifeguard and the ray of light bend their trajectory according to which path will take the least time, yet we ascribe a goal-oriented motivation to one, and not to the other.

Prof Tegmark further points out that the above example is not an exception, and that this is a common thread of observation in nature whereby, 'out of all the ways that nature could choose to do something it prefers the optimal way which typically boils down to minimizing or maximizing some quantity'.[2]

So, it appears that nature is always striving to optimize something. But precisely what is nature trying to optimize, and why should we care? Can the answer to this question provide insights into how societies and the business landscape unfold? I wondered if I could align my life and career goals with such 'natural' optimization principles, in order to maximize my chances of success. If there was a parallel between the behaviour of the lifeguard and a ray of light, what if I could find similar patterns in business, the economy and society?

Order and disorder

So what is nature trying to maximize? The universe appears to display two conflicting goals. The first goal of nature seems to be 'maximizing entropy'. Entropy is the measure of disorder in phenomena. When an entity reaches maximum entropy, it can no longer function, and it dies. A newborn baby is in a state of minimum entropy; as they grow up, their entropy levels increase. Eventually, when they die, their body disintegrates and their mind stops functioning. At this point, we say that they have reached a state of maximum entropy. According to what we know about the universe so far, it seems that since the moment of the Big Bang the universe has been getting messier and messier, going towards a state of complete entropy and destruction.

Does that sound like a depressing picture of the universe? Fortunately, nature appears to have a second goal, as described by the laws of physics: that 'random groups of particles strive to organize themselves so as to extract energy from their environment as effectively as possible'.[3] Nature's second goal can be described as the opposite of entropy – self-organization. Life, and intellectual life in particular, are the most effective manifestation of this second goal. By creating families, towns, countries and international organizations, humans have been able to create highly effective self-organized systems. As far as we know, we humans are the life forms that have been most successful in achieving this goal.

How inner and outer circles are created

So let's recap. So far, we know that life forms are continually trying to create systems (order), to overcome the effect of entropy (disorder). However, this effort causes one big problem, which can be explained by Schrödinger's observation that living systems maintain or reduce entropy (in themselves) by increasing the entropy around them.[4] What this means is that living systems strive to increase the level of order *within their inner circles*, by increasing the level of disorder and destruction in their *outer circles*. For example, animals eat other animals and plants to survive. In doing so, they maximize their survival (order) by causing destruction (disorder) in the world around them. Humans do the same. As our technologies have advanced, we've generated more and more damage to our environment.

DID YOU KNOW?

Nietzsche gives a metaphor for these two conflicting modes of life. He calls them Apollonian and Dionysian. Apollo was the mythological Greek god of order and form, and Dionysus was the opposing god of formlessness and disorder. Nietzsche celebrates a life where these two forces reach a balance. While Apollo brings order and predictability to life, Dionysus makes it unpredictable and more interesting, by keeping us on our toes.

So, if all of our seemingly profound goals can boil down to nature's struggle between order and disorder, what does it mean to our experience of life?

In our quest to find a balance between order and disorder, we create unique life experiences. The more skilful we become in doing this, the more happiness we will experience. When we lose the balance in favour of any of these forces, we suffer. On a personal level, this suffering manifests itself in terms of unhappiness and dissatisfaction. On a societal level, it turns into wars, and on a planetary level, it can threaten life on Earth.

If you think about the concept of order and disorder in the business landscape, it explains why disruption occurs and the role that technology plays in this process. Every time we create a new invention to improve our business processes, we disrupt a previous inner circle and its state of order. For example, steam power disrupted an earlier state of order, whereby physical work was done by muscle power and the aristocracy were in charge. Anyone who didn't belong to their inner circle had no real chance of improving their lives.

Then, steam power and subsequent technologies of the First and Second Industrial Revolutions disrupted the previous system and broke the inner circle of the aristocracy. More people found the opportunity to innovate and gain power, and education became more widespread. This created a new form of order and an inner circle of middle classes. The introduction of digital technologies once again disrupted the previous order and burst the existing inner circles. Thanks to these new technologies, we are now going through another transition in the business landscape, which inevitably impacts other aspects of our social, economic and political life. The critical thing to bear in mind here is that the speed of these transitions is increasing, and it's becoming harder to control their impact on our planet and our species.

Our planet

We affect our planet with almost every choice we make. Naturally, we are always trying to maximize our options. That's really what the quest for career success is all about. Whether we want to make a bigger impact, gain recognition or make more money, success ultimately comes down to having more choice on some level. Ironically, the more choices we have, the more we affect our planet.

As I write these words, I'm on a flight to Japan to speak at a conference. Sitting in business class means that I have more choices of food and more room to lie down and sleep if I need to. When I was very young, I didn't have any of these choices. I couldn't travel much further than in my hometown. That meant I had much less of a negative impact on the environment. My carbon footprint was much lower. I have managed to increase the order in my own life by increasing disorder and causing damage to the environment. At the same time, there are climate protests happening around the world, some of which are trying to stop aeroplanes from taking off. While I completely agree with their sentiment that we need to stop damaging our planet, I still really need to travel for my work. I'm not sure how I could do it otherwise. If we take a closer look at many other aspects of our lives, we will see that we affect our planet in many ways, which are not always as apparent as flying across the world.

Think about food. The ingredients in the food that you ate today were in a highly disorganized state, from different locations, perhaps hundreds of miles away. The supermarket brought the ingredients together and organized them onto the shelves, clearly labelled for you to find easily and effortlessly. By the time you *organize* those ingredients into a delicious meal, there will be many more steps involved. They need to be packaged and transported, and you will need to refrigerate them to keep them fresh. Chances are with all of those steps you are impacting the environment. The truth is that our technologies have grown faster than we have had an opportunity to consider and plan for their consequences.

Thanks to our ability to self-organize as a society, we humans have created processes to increase order and decrease disorder in accessing resources. However, in doing so, we have invariably increased the overall entropy of our planet and the atmosphere around it. In other words, we are always *thinking and acting locally*, but our actions often have *global implications*. We are continually creating processes to increase order in our inner circle. Still, in doing so, we affect our outer circles – often negatively. It's a little bit like cleaning your house by brushing all the rubbish under the carpet.

THE UNITED NATIONS' SUSTAINABLE DEVELOPMENT GOALS

There are those of us trying to expand our collective inner circles and fight against global entropy. Check out the 17 Sustainable Development Goals (SDGs) from the United Nations (UN) – these are specific goals that can be reduced to three main categories: economic equality, health and wellbeing, and environmental. Nearly all of human suffering in our world today can be solved if we overcome these three challenges.

Economic equality

It's hard to think about saving the planet and improving global health and wellbeing when you have more immediate financial concerns and career fear. Economic uncertainty can overshadow every aspect of life, from education to health, and even our sense of purpose, and it's difficult to worry about the outer circles of planet and species when you're preoccupied with worry about your inner circles of self and family. Besides, many experts agree that the answer to most of our global problems requires intervention on governmental and institutional levels, and this is not a book for policymakers – this is primarily a book for people like you and me who want to improve their lives, rather than sit back and wait for someone else to come up with solutions.

But – part of finding your place in the world is about seeing the bigger picture – knowing your place in the world, where we are and where we are headed. And, if I were to focus on just one of the key themes from the SDGs that could potentially help solve all the others, it would be economic empowerment. In my experience and observation, so much of human suffering stems from economic inequality. Economic empowerment is not only hugely relevant for combatting individual career fear, but as a global goal, it will enable more people to contribute to solving world problems.

That said, you may have your suspicions about whether things are getting better or worse in the global economy, and whether technology is going to benefit all of us equally. In the next section, we will explore the current economic state of the world. These economic challenges can affect all other areas in the 17 goals of the UN. They can also impact your next career move, massively.

The shrinking circle of economic growth

For the past three centuries since the start of the First Industrial Revolution, we have seen considerable improvements to humans' living conditions. Thanks to technological advancements, almost every nation is better off today in terms of both economy and healthcare. Even developing countries have benefited from this economic prosperity, in comparison to a few centuries ago. Although they may still be far behind the majority of developed countries in many respects, they have experienced real growth in comparison to their past.

It's natural to think that this growth and improvement will steadily continue. Even some highly respected economists such as Donald Boudreaux and Mark Perry have argued that technology will continue to improve our living conditions and create economic growth.[5] However, many of our old established economic paradigms haven't caught up with the digital economy: technology is growing faster than we have the infrastructure to deal with its implications. While, on the surface, it may look as if the GDP (gross domestic product – the sum total of what a country has produced in monetary terms) of technologically advanced countries shows an overall growth, this doesn't automatically guarantee equal economic progress for everyone.

In their brilliant book *The Second Machine Age*, Professor Erik Brynjolfsson and Andrew McAfee demonstrate that while the output or product of technological growth has increased, so has the gap between those who make the most and those who make the least. In the United States, for example, although the overall GDP has continued to rise in the past century, the income of the median US household peaked in 1999, as it reached $54,932.[6] This means that after 1999, the average American has become poorer overall in real terms. And the median income has continued to fall: in 2011, this figure was $50,054 – 10 per cent lower than at the start of the 21st century. How could this be? Well, it turns out that the overall GDP growth is attributed to the top 10 per cent of Americans who earned more than half the total income, and to the top 1 per cent who earned over 22 per cent of the income.[7] A similar trend is visible in other developed countries.

Erik and Andy explain that before the digital revolution of the 1990s, there was a direct correlation between productivity and employment. On a national level, productivity is measured in terms of GDP, which shows the average output level of a country, per head. In the past, economists estimated a nation's relative degree of prosperity based on its GDP. But since the digital revolution, there has been a decoupling of productivity and employment – employment rates and GDP are no longer directly linked the way they used to be. In real terms, digital natives (such as millennials and younger generations) are likely to feel the real-life impact of this decoupling, as they are those making up the majority of workers – and the impact will only be felt more when we consider the effects of artificial intelligence and machine learning that we looked at in previous chapters.

The winner-takes-all economies

So, we've considered what our place in the world is on a universal level, and on a global level, and focused in on economic equality as the global factor most relevant to battling both global injustice and individual career fear. The final piece of the puzzle, then, is to look at the current economic landscape, and consider how we might fit into *that*, both now and in the future. In the above examples, we looked at GDP – the internationally agreed metric by which we compare and discuss productivity on a national level. Many economists still emphasize GDP as a measure of a country's prosperity. However, there are two main problems with this approach.

The tangible and the intangible

The first problem with GDP is that it measures only tangible assets and output that can be expressed quantifiably. This means that it fails to consider the value of intangible assets, such as intellectual property, algorithms, ideas and so on.

For example, before we had the internet and streaming services, music sales contributed to GDP, since people bought vinyl, cassettes and CDs. Today, many artists give their songs away for free or make them available through streaming services. Between 2004 and 2008 the revenue from sales of music dropped by 40 per cent, from $12.3 billion to $7.4 billion.[8] The value of music hasn't decreased, but it's not generating as much money for the artists and the economy. Artists now need to find other ways to supplement their income. The songs have become almost a free token.

The same story is true for other forms of media, content and entertainment. Over the past few years, many magazines and newspapers have shut down. Some have gone digital, and some have completely disappeared. People are consuming more content than ever, but they are not necessarily paying for it. For example, I put a tremendous amount of effort into my content on LinkedIn and other social media, but I don't monetize it directly. I even invested tens of thousands of pounds into making a documentary that I then released for free. Instead, I've built an ecosystem of by-products around it.

Now, you could say that my content is an intangible asset for me. That is true, but not everyone sees it as such. My bank won't give me a business loan because of my LinkedIn followers, and my mortgage provider doesn't care about how much money I put into my documentary. You can't buy a meal with your content, or with your social media followers and your engagement. While a new economy of influencer marketing has emerged, it's still minimal in comparison to the level of income that media and entertainment used to generate in the past.

Most importantly, the real beneficiaries of the content that musicians, artists and content creators put out for free or for minimal return are the platforms that host them. This brings me to the second problem of GDP. With the advent of the internet and the digital economy, GDP is no longer a good representation of the ordinary income of society. Instead, we are quickly moving towards a winner-takes-all economy. Here are a couple of examples.

Example 1: The platform economy

Every time you post on any social media, you are benefiting that platform directly, regardless of whether you are a professional content creator or simply posting your holiday photos. Just by being there and posting your content, you are creating direct value for the platform. Some people may make money from their content, but the truth is that this includes only a fraction of any platform's users. Remember the discussion about influencer culture in Chapter 2? Only a tiny percentage of content creators can make a living from their content. However, every single user generates value for the platform by enriching their data. As of this writing, Facebook has over two billion users; Instagram, over one billion; and LinkedIn boasts over 600 million users. How many platforms of that size are out there? Not that many – and therein lies their value.

But the platform economy doesn't end with social networks. Think about marketplaces for goods and services, such as Amazon, eBay, Fiverr and Upwork. Even companies like Uber and Airbnb are essentially built on this new platform or network economy. Platforms don't even necessarily need to have their own physical assets; instead, they can facilitate the distribution of *other people's* assets and connect buyers and sellers, or content creators and the audience. In the process, they gain massive amounts of data, which, as we discussed before, is the most valuable commodity of our time. I tend to think about this new digital economy in a similar way to the business model of a casino. Everyone goes there to play. Some people win, and some lose, but the overall winner is always the house.

Another thing to consider is that almost all of these platforms encourage a further winner-takes-all economy, even *within* the platform. For example, Amazon's rating systems and detailed feedback of customers about the products are a massive part of what makes Amazon special. It adds huge value to the platform. The same applies to the feedback and rating systems on eBay, Airbnb, Uber and many freelancer platforms; these ratings benefit customers, but they can also push the vendors to compromise massively on their price to stay competitive and put themselves under immense pressure to achieve a higher rating. If you are not among the top 1 per cent in any category, you may not get a chance to be seen by potential buyers who want their orders quickly and cheaply. In this model, the customers benefit, and the vendors often operate with immense pressure. Still, the real winners are the platform owners.

In the meantime, traditional business models in most industries are suffering, and many of them are going out of business. Think about the music stores, bookshops and many shopping malls and fashion brands that vanished thanks to the likes of Amazon, Spotify and online clothing brands. As I write this section, I'm on my way back from Japan, where I gave a talk about the impact of technology on the future of the travel industry. One of the most talked-about subjects at this convention was the demise of the giant travel company, Thomas Cook. Close to 10,000 people lost their jobs, and people donated money and food vouchers to the affected families. Now, Airbnb hires only a fraction of the staff of all the traditional travel companies combined. Still, for now, they are thriving in this new economy.

You may say that Thomas Cook had many other internal problems. You could say the same about Toys R Us, Debenhams, Maplin and many other retailers that filed for bankruptcy in the past few years, while the digital economy has been thriving. The correlation is undeniable.

While we benefit from these platforms and enjoy the convenience that they bring us, the real winners of this new economy are a small number of tech giants. So, as you think about your future career, this is something to consider.

Example 2: Job-eating algorithms

There was a time when people went to university to study photography and filmmaking. Those university degrees still exist. Still, I have difficulty seeing how a career in those fields can be sustainable in the next decade. Over the past decade of being a filmmaker, I have seen my industry going from being one of the best paid for freelancers to one of the lowest paid. Only the best of the best seem to be still able to demand high wages.

I usually have a camera operator accompanying me to conferences to help create short vlogs about the experience. This time, at the travel convention in Japan, I had to film myself, and I didn't want to be carrying around a bulky DSLR. So, I decided to use my phone camera. As a filmmaker, I used to be super-snobbish about using smartphone cameras, but I was surprised at how I managed to get great shots using mine. The phone's camera shows a clear difference even from the previous model from only a year ago. The stabilization, wide-angle lens and autofocus are insanely good. It's hard to believe that until last year, I would have had to pay hundreds of dollars per day for someone to achieve the same results. No doubt, by the time you read this book, the camera capability of your smartphone will put mine to shame. How does the phone camera achieve this? Through algorithms that tell it how to adjust its settings in different lighting and movement situations – tasks that would previously have been performed by skilled individuals.

When the quality of our smartphone cameras is coupled with the convenience of sharing them with the world through social media, this has dramatic effects on the economy. Andy and Erik give startling statistics about the economic impacts of digital photography. They point out that analogue photography peaked in the year 2000, before it saw a decline. The pre-digital photography 'behemoth' Kodak employed 145,300 people. And yet, a team of only 15 people created the Instagram app, which they sold to Facebook for over $1 billion. In that same year, Kodak filed for bankruptcy after 132 years.[9]

Instagram has made a small number of people very rich, but it hasn't created middle-class jobs for over 145,000 people as Kodak did. While the overall income of Facebook and Instagram add to the GDP, they are not creating equal economic opportunities for as many people. This story is not unique to the film and photography industry. The digital economy and job-eating algorithms will continue to affect almost every industry.

Your next step in finding your place in the world

We will end this chapter by answering two critical questions. Exactly which jobs will be affected, and what can you do about it?

Well, the truth is that most professions are likely to see a partial decline in at least half of the tasks that constitute them. The tell-tale signs of functions that are likely to be disrupted are repetitive tasks that can be defined in terms of the 'IF... + THEN ...' formula. These are often tasks that don't require any of the uniquely human skills that we're going to look at next.

As for what you can do about it: whether you run your own business or work in a company, there are four innately human skills that will help you navigate your way in the age of artificial intelligence and the digital economy. These are:

- emotional intelligence;
- contextual creativity;
- critical thinking; and
- mindfulness.

In the next four chapters, we will explore each of those skills in much more detail to help you navigate your way as you get to know yourself and find your place in the world. And the best part of this is that all of those skills are completely learnable! You don't have to be born with them; I've been teaching myself for a very long time. I've got better at some of them quicker, and some have been more challenging. But even limited progress in those areas has helped me massively in navigating my career through technological disruptions. They've also helped me expand my inner circle and find areas where I can contribute and inspire others to do the same. This gives me a sense of purpose and drives me to keep growing. I hope it will do the same for you.

Endnotes

1   Tegmark, M (2018) *Life 3.0: Being human in the age of artificial intelligence*, p 250, Penguin Books, London

2   Tegmark, M (2018) *Life 3.0: Being human in the age of artificial intelligence*, p 251, Penguin Books, London

3   Tegmark, M (2018) *Life 3.0: Being human in the age of artificial intelligence*, p 252, Penguin Books, London. Prof Tegmark explains that this fact is based on Erwin Schrödinger's powerful 1944 book, *What Is Life? The physical aspect of the living cell*, Cambridge University Press, Cambridge

4   Schrödinger, E (1992) *What Is Life? The physical aspect of the living cell*, Cambridge University Press, Cambridge

5   Boudreaux, D J (2013) Donald Boudreaux and Mark Perry: The Myth of a Stagnant Middle Class, *Wall Street Journal*, 23 January, www.wsj.com/articles/SB10001424127887323468604578249723138161566 (archived at https://perma.cc/73T5-XKCH)

6   Brynjolfsson, E and McAfee, A (2016) *The Second Machine Age: Work, progress, and prosperity in a time of brilliant technologies*, WW Norton & Company, New York

7   Brynjolfsson, E and McAfee, A (2016) *The Second Machine Age: Work, progress, and prosperity in a time of brilliant technologies*, ch 11, WW Norton & Company, New York

8   Brynjolfsson, E and McAfee, A (2016) *The Second Machine Age: Work, progress, and prosperity in a time of brilliant technologies*, ch 8, WW Norton & Company, New York

9   Brynjolfsson, E and McAfee, A (2016) *The Second Machine Age: Work, progress, and prosperity in a time of brilliant technologies*, ch 8, WW Norton & Company, New York

PART THREE

(Human) skills

So far, we've looked at how to know ourselves and how to find our place in the world by defining and expanding our inner circles. Hopefully, this has helped us gain perspective and adopt the right mindset for future career success. Now, let's look at the four essential – and uniquely human – skills that will help us navigate our way.

One of the most significant points of concern about the future of work is about the contrast between skills that machines can replicate, and those that are innately human. Today, machines can accomplish tasks that even a few years ago we may not have thought possible – we saw this pattern repeat itself in Part One on the history of work. We always have to take this into account and never get complacent, thinking that they will not be able to catch up with us in these areas. We may have to prepare to redefine these human skills continually. I would argue that we must be prepared even to redefine what it means to be human.

So, with that in mind, the four uniquely human skills needed for career success in the foreseeable future are *emotional intelligence*, *critical thinking*, *contextual creativity* and *mindfulness*. All of these four skills have an emergent property – the output of each skill is greater than the sum of its parts. As we saw in Chapter 3, when we looked at the difference between emotional processing and logic, this is what makes these skills different from how machines operate.

CHAPTER SEVEN

Emotional intelligence

One of the pioneers of this field, Daniel Goleman, describes emotional intelligence as 'the ability to motivate oneself and persist in the face of frustrations, to control impulse, and delay gratification; to regulate one's moods and keep distress from swamping the ability to think, to empathize, and to hope.'[1] You can see why this skill could be hugely important to our career success. All of those abilities are critical for beating career fear.

Emotional intelligence is often contrasted with IQ, or intelligence quotient, which has more to do with our logical, spatial and linguistic abilities. Measuring someone's IQ is a lot more straightforward than measuring their EI (or EQ). There are well-established tests for IQ measurement, which take about half a day to complete. IQ is not enough for life and career success, though. To succeed, we need general intelligence, which we talked about in Part One of this book – this is what separates us from machines right now. A huge part of general intelligence is emotional intelligence, which is what this chapter is all about.

Why is emotional intelligence so important?

Emotional intelligence is connected to our subjective experience; it is unlikely that machines will be able to gain emotional intelligence without subjective experience. This gives us humans an edge (for now). However, as we will see, there is a close relationship between emotional and logical intelligence, and we can't get complacent.

Our logical processing is already 'disrupted' and enhanced by computers. Just as steam power both enhanced and disrupted jobs at the beginning of the Industrial Revolution, computers are doing the same for us today, although at a much faster rate.

As humans, we have three primary abilities to fall back on: physical, cognitive and emotional. When steam power disrupted physical labour, we turned to our cognitive skills – knowledge workers rose to the top. Now computers are disrupting knowledge work. The question is, can we fall back on our emotional intelligence?

I say yes! When the Industrial Revolution happened, we had nowhere near as much knowledge as we have today. Within just a few centuries, we enhanced our logical education and abilities massively. Many people who were traditionally engaged in physical work for centuries had to gain new skills and knowledge. Now, we have to do the same for our emotional intelligence.

How to measure emotional intelligence?

Because emotions, and emotional intelligence, are subjective, they are very difficult to measure. However, there are a few different ways of conceptualizing emotional intelligence; here are three of the best known.

MSCEIT (MAYER–SALOVEY–CARUSO EMOTIONAL INTELLIGENCE TEST)
One of the most respected researched-based studies of EI is called MSCEIT. Three academics from Yale University created this model:

Mayor, Salovey and Caruso. They have a four-branch model of emotional intelligence that breaks the concept down into:

1 perception and expression of emotion;
2 using emotions and thought;
3 understanding and analysing emotions;
4 managing emotions in yourself and others.

You can take the official MSCEIT test online at MHS.com, for a fee.

BAR-ON APPROACH

This model of measuring and defining emotional intelligence takes an approach based on one's personality traits. For example, it argues that if you are high in extroversion or neuroticism, this could affect your emotional intelligence. To me, this makes a lot of sense, as there is a close relationship between our personality traits and how we perceive emotions or behave towards other people.

A reliable test in this category is the Schutte Self-Report Emotional Intelligence Test (SSEIT), which you can find through Google Scholar.

GOLEMAN'S EI MODEL

Daniel Goleman has developed another approach to advancing and measuring EI. His approach has been particularly popular in the context of workplace environments. Goleman explains that the value of emotional intelligence is in three critical areas: *understanding yourself, understanding others* and finally *having the ability to take (the right) action*.[2] I find this conceptualization the most straightforward of the three popular approaches to emotional intelligence, although, in principle, they all have a lot in common.

Goleman's EI test is called the Emotional and Social Competence Inventory (ESCI), and you can find it online, again for a fee.

FINDING THE RIGHT EI (OR EQ) TEST

The terms EI and EQ are often used interchangeably. If you are looking for the tests online and come across either of those terms, they are talking about the same thing. So, how can you find a *reliable* and *valid* test to measure your EI, especially if you are looking for free tests online? You need to be aware of three essential criteria:

1   How the test environment affects your responses. Taking the test in the presence of others could affect your answers, for example.

2   Are the questions clearly explained, or do they mix up two or more subjects? You don't want a test that has a lot of jargon.

3   Are there enough questions to avoid sampling errors? For example, if a test claims to measure your EI with just half a dozen questions, you have to question its reliability.

TESTING ACCURACY

Tests such as those mentioned above can be helpful places to start, but it's worth bearing in mind that they do have their limitations, especially with such a subjective concept as EI. For example, most EI tests are survey-based, which can be a problem: it means that the tests are relying on your own answers to make a judgement, and it is notoriously difficult to self-assess accurately.

Here's a made-up example of the kind of question or scenario that you may be faced with in an EI test. The questions may include images of people with different facial expressions and backstories, and the test may ask you to guess what the person is thinking, or how you think they should respond to a given situation.

EI Test: Example   In Figure 7.1 we can see Jason, Martin, Zack and Andrew. Here's the scenario: Jason has just been promoted.

FIGURE 7.1 EI test example

Andrew was up for the same promotion, but he didn't get it. Zack and Martin are junior associates who work with both Jason and Andrew.

Now try answering the following questions:

- Based on his facial expression, how is Jason feeling?
  1 He is feeling smug and is rubbing Andrew's face in it.
  2 He is feeling proud of his accomplishment; he is oblivious about how Andrew might be feeling.
  3 He is thinking about Andrew's feelings and how to cheer him up.
- How do you think Andrew should behave towards Jason now?
  1 It is natural for him to feel jealous because he believes he deserved the promotion.
  2 He should be happy for Jason and think about how he can learn from him.
  3 He should go around the office and tell everyone that he deserved the promotion.

What did you decide? I'll bet that many of you chose answer 3 and answer 2, respectively – these are probably the most obvious 'favourable' responses. However, it's much easier to give favourable responses when you know you are being tested, and have time to think. If you were involved in this situation in real life, most of us would probably find it much harder to put our EI knowledge into practice, because life and work situations can be a lot more complicated. It's much easier to say that an imaginary someone passed over for a promotion should try to feel happy for, and learn from, their competitor, than it is to feel that way when getting passed over for a promotion yourself! This is an example of what we might call self-reporting bias, and is an important limitation in many EI tests.

Then too, many of these tests can create a false binary. In this imaginary story, as in many real-life situations, it often comes down to a question of who's right – but is that always the best question to ask?

Who's right? Truth and validity

In the story of Jason and Andrew, they both felt that they deserved a promotion, but one got it and the other one didn't. We need both Jason and Andrew to understand themselves and each other in order to be able to communicate with each other with emotional intelligence.

Understanding yourself takes lifelong practice and is a massive task in itself – we looked at it in a little detail in Part Two of this book, but it's an iterative process of ongoing self-reflection. As hard as truly understanding yourself can be, understanding others can be magnitudes more difficult. What makes it uniquely challenging is that they both rely on subjective experience. Now, *your* subjective experience may be very different from someone else's, and that's where things go wrong.

Human communication can be incredibly complex and challenging to navigate. Conflict arises from a lack of agreement on who is right – in our example, Jason feels that he is right, in that he deserved the promotion and Andrew should be happy for him, but Andrew feels he is right in that he deserved the promotion and Jason should recognize this. And so it goes in all conflicts: in each situation, both parties feel that *their* experience is real and accurate, but their truths don't always match.

Remember in Chapter 3, when we looked at the difference between the truth and the validity of a statement? Truth is based on subjective experience from a single point of view – this can be the viewpoint of a person or a group. By definition, a statement can't be true from two opposing points of view. If two people both perceive the same truth, they belong to the same group or 'inner circle' *on that topic*.

People, organizations and even countries clash because they can't agree on the same 'truth'. Often, though, neither side is willing to question the 'validity' of their version of the truth.

The way to move past conflict, be able to communicate and reach a resolution is to try to match our truth to those of others, and understand where they are coming from. That's what we call empathy, which is one of the building blocks of emotional intelligence. Instead of focusing on who is right and who is wrong, empathy focuses on where the two viewpoints might overlap. Let's now look at the concept of empathy and its close cousin, sympathy. Whenever I talk about empathy, I notice that some people mix it up with sympathy.

Empathy vs sympathy

Empathy is having the ability to put yourself in another's shoes and see a situation from their point of view, imagining how they may feel and (to a certain extent) feeling those emotions along with them. *Sympathy* is a feeling of sorrow, pity or compassion for someone else – but the concept can be problematic, as it highlights the divide between people. Imagine that you tell me that you have the flu and are feeling really poorly; if I have sympathy for you, I may express how sorry for you I am feeling, I may tell you to get well soon... and I may also be thinking that

I am glad I don't have the flu, or wondering if perhaps you are exaggerating how poorly you are, or simply feeling compassion for you without necessarily being moved to any action. Maybe you sense this on some level, and maybe you hate the feeling of being pitied – and the divide between us is emphasized.

If, on the other hand, I can think about when I have had the flu – I remember how dreadful I felt, how poorly I was, and how I wasn't able to function normally for a good couple of weeks – then I can empathize with you. I can remember how I felt, and use that information to imagine how you must be feeling now. This might stir me into action – perhaps I'll bring you medicine and soup, if we're good friends, or tell you not to worry about work until you're much better, if we work together. I may express these feelings to you, telling you how dreadful I felt when I had the flu, and you may feel less alone, and reassured that I do understand. In effect, the divide between us is diminished, and we have found common ground.

Developing empathy

Empathy is a crucial building block of our EI skills. Having empathy is a fundamental step in being able to move an argument from subjective 'truth' to 'validity', and looking at it with a clear mind. You need to know what is 'true' to you, and you need to empathize with and understand what is 'true' for the other party. Only then can you gauge the validity of either of your points of view.

Let's consider a workplace example: say your boss thinks that you could be delivering a project much faster than you currently do. You may feel that your boss is unreasonable and that they shouldn't expect you to work more quickly than you are comfortable doing. Perhaps you think you need three days to finish a project, but they expect you to deliver it in one day.

You could allow yourself to get agitated and stressed out under pressure, which could make things a lot worse and create a bad feeling in your workplace. Alternatively, you could choose to remain calm and put yourself in your boss's shoes: perhaps they are under pressure from their own supervisors or clients. Maybe they believe that you are more capable than you think you are, and they want to help you progress faster: you can choose to see this as a positive point and take on the challenge to learn new techniques and shortcuts.

How you react depends on your ability to put yourself in your boss's shoes and understand where they're coming from. You need to be able to get an accurate picture of what they're *really* saying, and understand why it makes you feel the way it does. Finally, you need to be able to respond calmly and compassionately. When we break down this process, we get *feeling*, *understanding* and *action*.

Remember this from Goleman's EI model? Almost every situation involving emotional intelligence has those three components. For example, you may be preparing for a job interview and you feel incredibly nervous. You can ask the following questions to understand your feelings better and decide what to do about it:

Feeling:
Q: How am I feeling?
A: I am feeling nervous.

Understanding:
Q: Why am I feeling nervous?
A: Because I'm worried that I may not get the job – a future possibility that hasn't yet happened, and so I still have time to do something about it.

Action:
Q: What can I do to improve my chances of getting the job?
A: I can research the company and the job I'm applying for, so I can demonstrate a good understanding of their business. I

can practise some of the skills that are important to them and show that I'm passionate and willing to learn.

All of a sudden, you have more options and things don't look so bad! As you see, the three components of *feeling*, *understanding* and *action* are not just about your interaction with others. They also determine how you keep yourself motivated and stay positive and optimistic in stressful situations. So, let's take a closer look at these components and see why they can sometimes be challenging to get right.

How our brain 'captures' reality

Feelings or emotions are impulses rooted in our evolutionary biology. These impulses are formulated by elementary sensations designed by evolution to help us survive. You may have heard of the term 'alligator brain' or 'lizard brain': this is the oldest part of the human brain, nicknamed because the theory is that humans have this neurology in common with early evolutionary reptilian ancestors. When we talk about *emotions*, imagine the reptilian brain, and when we talk about *understanding*, think of the human brain. (Please note: these are metaphors! Neurologists don't always agree on breaking down the brain into specific regions where feeling and thinking happen – but it can be a helpful analogy, so for now we'll go with it.)

We have previously used the analogy of colours and colour grading in photography when talking about personality traits in Chapter 5. I'll build on that same analogy here to help us grasp how emotions work and how to understand and regulate them. Think about the reptilian and the human brain as two photographers.

One of them is well trained and equipped with the latest technologies. They have an eye for detail, their composition is precise and their photos are white-balanced correctly. They also make excellent use of complex colours such as magenta and cyan. Most importantly, they know where, in an image, to focus their lens, and their pictures are sharp and crisp. But they also know that they have to take their time to capture a great image; they can't rush things. This photographer is the human brain.

Our other photographer, however, is self-taught and not very sophisticated. They just about get by. They don't recognize the complexity of colours, and only know the primary shades of red, green and blue (RGB). Their pictures are often out of focus, and their white balance is usually off. They're also in a hurry and don't take the time to compose their images properly. They're good at specific tasks, though. For example, they generally have a good sense of direction. They also *love* their job and are super-passionate. This photographer is our reptilian brain.

Now, every event that happens in our lives is a scene that needs to be captured in our brain before we can respond to it. Every instant in life, every moment that we call 'now', is like a still image. The two photographers in our brain have to work together to help us capture an accurate representation of that event before we can respond to it. So why can't we dispense with the reptilian brain and let our human brain do all the 'photography'?

We can't get rid of either one of these photographers. They are bound together through evolution. They need each other to help us succeed and thrive. Neither one of them can thrive on their own. They find meaning in their opposition. The trick is to create a balance between them, and that balance starts with capturing our emotions correctly.

How to know how you are feeling

As humans, we have many complex emotions: some languages and cultures have thousands of names for them. For the sake of simplicity, let's agree that for our purposes, our most basic emotions can be characterized as anger, disgust, joy, fear and sadness. Those five basic emotions are like primary colours: you can mix them and get many different shades.

Our reptilian brain is mainly tuned into those five basic emotions; it doesn't always have the ability to distinguish more complex shades of emotion. Most importantly, it's not always sure *why* it feels the way it does. The reptilian brain is designed to act fast. It is mighty because it's had a tremendous amount of practice in capturing images with basic emotions. The pictures might be blurry with poor colour balance, but they've been good enough to help us survive until now. In the wild, our ancestors had to react to the dangers of their environment instantly. When another animal approached you, you had a split second to decide whether it was lunch or whether you were going to be its lunch. In this situation, a blurry and off-balance picture was often all you needed to decide how to react. If you waited too long to take the perfect picture, you risked being eaten.

In the 21st century, we are no longer facing life-and-death situations daily, as our ancestors did. Our societies have become more complex and sophisticated, and our reptilian brain is unable to capture the intricacy of modern communication. But we often default to using this ancient 'photographer' in our brain. They are so passionate that they jump ahead and dominate most situations before our human brain has an opportunity to take out their 'camera'.

For example, imagine you are on your way to the airport and well on track to make it in time for your flight. Suddenly there is an accident on the road that slows you down. Your reptilian brain may quickly take over and highjack all of your thinking. It can make you anxious, and you will start to think of all the worst-case scenarios if you lose your flight.

For the reptilian brain, almost every situation is a matter of survival. Missing your flight is never a pleasant situation to be in, but it's not as bad as being eaten alive by a bear. When my reptilian 'photographer' highjacks a scene, I can feel momentarily paralysed, until my human brain kicks in and takes a more accurate picture of the situation. Then, I can reformulate things and find a solution.

Having the ability to recognize precisely what it is that you are feeling is important. If I ask you to describe your feeling at any given time, you are likely to mention one of the basic feelings of 'joy, sadness, anger, fear and disgust'. But if I keep probing you to dig deeper into any of those emotions, you will be able to unpack more complex shades underneath. This will help you get a more accurate picture of exactly how you feel and why. Then you can decide if your image needs adjusting.

Sometimes we feel certain emotions too strongly, and other times they may be darker or too pastel. When I worked in TV, we had a process for monitoring videos before they went on air to make sure that none of the colours went beyond a certain level of safety for human vision. They called it 'broadcast safe'. Those of us who feel emotions too strongly may need to put a broadcast-safe limit before we project them onto the world. Conversely, if we struggle to feel passionate and motivated, we need to let more light and intensity into our lives. All this emotional adjustment takes a lot of work, though, and it's never easy. It takes self-control and conscious effort, which is what we will turn to next.

Self-control

In his course 'Scientific secrets for self-control', Professor Nathan DeWall defines self-control as the ability 'to override an impulse so that you can agree with a standard for what's appropriate.'[3] He goes on to explain that there are three parts to the process of self-control. First, you feel an urge to do something or think about it. Next, you feel a desire to override that urge. Finally, by overriding that urge, you've adhered to a standard.

A 'standard' is an objective reference point for what's appropriate.[4] For example, if you see a delicious-looking box of doughnuts sitting on a desk in your office, your brain might say, go ahead and have one, two or half a dozen of them. That's the urge emotion! But you know that the delicious doughnuts aren't yours to take, so you walk on past: that's overriding the urge. Although your body is encouraging you to eat the doughnuts, you stop yourself from doing so, because A) you have agreed to a standard of possession of goods and that stealing is wrong, and B) you have developed good enough self-control to stop yourself from indulging.

These three parts are essentially what we talked about earlier, 'feeling, understanding and action'. Your reptilian brain drives the desire for the doughnuts. It says: 'Eat, eat as much as you can while there is food. You may not get any food for days after this! The next jungle is miles away, and you could starve by the time we get there!'

Then, self-control kicks in. Here, your human brain says: 'Hang on a minute; we are not in the jungles anymore. We are in the 21st century, at the heart of civilization. There is no lack of calories here, and I'm not going to starve. Plus, these doughnuts don't belong to me.'

Doing the right thing sounds so easy when you put it that way. So, outside of this nice and simple engineered example... why is self-control so *hard* sometimes? Well, it turns out that much of it comes down to energy.

Self-control energy

The battle between the reptilian brain and the human brain can be exhausting. By the time your *feelings* and *understanding* have an internal committee inside your mind, you'll have used up some of your *self-control energy*. Understanding and deciding on the right action is one thing; making yourself do it is another. Once you know what to do, you still need more self-control to make yourself adhere to it. Understanding is not enough; action is what counts. I can't tell you the number of times I've given in to my impulses and taken the wrong action even if I understood that it was wrong. Sometimes you know you are making a mistake, but by then you may have run out of energy to do the right thing.

Professor DeWall explains that there are several theories on exactly how self-control works. One of the most accepted theories, and the one that resonates best with my own experience, is that our mind functions as an energy system, and that self-control relies on this energy. To operate with restraint, you need to exert so much energy. The more you use this energy, the more depleted you become. Just as we need physical energy and psychological motivation to practise an instrument or play a sport, we need those same resources to develop self-control and emotional intelligence.

Physical strength

As we've seen, self-control can deplete your energy, just like learning any other skill does. So what can you do to make sure you have enough power? The answer is much more straightforward than you might think: eat and sleep properly. Honestly, it is often just that simple! Without self-control, your emotional intelligence goes out of the window, and without breakfast, your self-control follows it.

Studies show that people are far more likely to have self-control when they are well fed and not too tired. For example, in one study, experimenters engaged the participants in an activity that depleted their energy. They then split them into three groups and gave them a puzzle to solve. Unbeknown to the participants, the puzzle was unsolvable. The experimenters gave the first group a great-tasting milkshake, the second group a not so great-tasting drink (but with a similar amount of calories), and the third group were given a drink with no calories. The first and second group both persisted much longer in trying to solve the puzzle, while the third group, who were depleted by then, gave up much quicker. Similar experiments on both animals and humans have shown, time and again, that physical energy can have a massive impact on our ability to maintain self-control.[5] Sara Milne Rowe, the author of *The SHED Method*, explains all the critical physical conditions that can impact our self-control.

She talks about sleep, hydration, exercise and diet, and their impact on regulating our body, mood, mind, purpose and interaction with other people.[6]

But self-control is not a purely physical skill – there is another aspect to the strength and energy you need for emotional intelligence.

Psychological strength

The second aspect of developing the self-control muscle relies on our psychological strength. Just like our body needs food and sleep, our minds need a constant reminder of our values and purpose in life. This second aspect has been a massive point of strength for me in developing the emotional skills to propel my career to date: without the daily reminder of my purpose and values, I would have never made it to this point. To find your purpose and values, you have to define your inner and outer circles and determine your place in the world where you can contribute. Every time you feel frustrated with a situation, or you are about to give in to your impulses, think about where your values are.

From the moment that we wake up in the morning to the moment we go to bed, there are hundreds of instances per day that test our emotional intelligence. These moments of trial present many opportunities for us to improve our EI skills. Every time you feel happy, proud, jealous or anxious throughout the day, that's an opportunity for you to practise your emotional intelligence.

The action we take in any given situation is partly about the story we tell ourselves about what *really* happened. The second part is about knowing the right thing to do. For me, this has always come down to aiming to increase human happiness and decrease human suffering. In Chapter 10, we will look at some of the specific techniques that you can use for daily practice of sharpening this skill.

EI and technology

Do you think that modern technologies have made us more, or less, emotionally intelligent?

Several studies show that our reliance on modern technologies might be making us less emotionally intelligent. This is ironic, perhaps, because I would argue that we *need* EI to thrive in the age of modern technologies. Yet these same technologies could reduce our EI if we misuse them.

Jennifer Aaker of Stanford University 'analysed 72 studies performed on nearly 14,000 college students between 1979 and 2009. She found a sharp decline in empathy.'[7] Daniel Goleman also warns about the impact of social media on our relationships. He notes that social channels provide enough 'weak links' in our relationships that we may not bother forming 'strong links'.[8]

Part of this is because of the non-face-to-face nature of many of these tools and channels. When communicating via our screens, through text messages, e-mails or social media comments, we can't always see other people's facial expression or hear their tone of voice; this affects both the feeling and the understanding aspects of our interactions. If you can't read the other person's expressions, it becomes more difficult to understand their point of view and respond with empathy – the information you're receiving from them becomes limited.

But it's not that straightforward. I simply don't believe that modern communication technology, phones and social media, are inherently bad for us. The problem, in my opinion, is not necessarily with the tools themselves, but in *how we use them*. For example, I use LinkedIn to initiate relationships with other industry leaders. Later, I invite some of them to my thought-leadership events so I can get to know them better. I have found this to be a fantastic way to develop and invest in both my career and my professional network, and without a negative impact on my emotional intelligence.

So, what should we do? Well, I have found that one of the simplest ways of overcoming the challenge of communication in the age of digital technologies is to limit their use to situations that are less emotionally charged. If you are feeling a strong emotion before sending that text or e-mail or posting that comment, it's probably a sign that you should wait. Wait until you calm down, and speak to the other party in person.

In short, we don't yet know enough about the exact impact of modern technologies on our EQ. There have not been enough studies because these technologies are very new; so, in the meantime, we need to be a lot more mindful of our digital communications.

Endnotes

1 Goleman, D (2014) *Emotional Intelligence*, p 10, Bloomsbury Publishing, London

2 Goleman, D (2014) *Emotional Intelligence*, Bloomsbury Publishing, London

3 DeWall, C N (2019) Why Is It So Hard to Do What We Should? The Great Courses Plus, Track 1, www.thegreatcoursesplus.com/scientific-secrets-for-self-control/why-is-it-so-hard-to-do-what-we-should (archived at https://perma.cc/B4HU-TUMZ)

4 DeWall, C N (2019) Why Is It So Hard to Do What We Should? The Great Courses Plus, Track 1, www.thegreatcoursesplus.com/scientific-secrets-for-self-control/why-is-it-so-hard-to-do-what-we-should (archived at https://perma.cc/B4HU-TUMZ)

5 DeWall, C N (2019) Why Is It So Hard to Do What We Should? The Great Courses Plus, www.thegreatcoursesplus.com/scientific-secrets-for-self-control/why-is-it-so-hard-to-do-what-we-should (archived at https://perma.cc/B4HU-TUMZ)

6 Rowe, S M (2018) *The SHED Method: Making better choices when it matters*, Michael Joseph, London

7 Satterfield, J M (2019) Boosting Your Emotional Intelligence, The Great Courses Plus, Track 24, www.thegreatcoursesplus.com/show/boosting_your_emotional_intelligence (archived at https://perma.cc/6FW4-D9Z4)

8 Satterfield, J M (2019) Boosting Your Emotional Intelligence, The Great Courses Plus, Track 24, www.thegreatcoursesplus.com/show/boosting_your_emotional_intelligence (archived at https://perma.cc/6FW4-D9Z4)

CHAPTER EIGHT

Critical thinking

In the previous chapter on emotional intelligence we saw that there was a close relationship between feeling, thinking and our actions. In this and the next chapter, we will continue on the same path, and follow the same train of thought. Critical thinking – a skill highly related to and linked with emotional intelligence – becomes super-important in our career paths when it comes to decision making. Making good decisions requires understanding probability and prioritizing in our goal setting. It's a prerequisite to taking the right actions to achieve our goals.

But what exactly *is* critical thinking? The 'critical' part of critical thinking comes from the term 'crisis'.

When I say the word crisis, what's the first thing that comes to mind? Perhaps an earthquake, a political turmoil or a difficult personal situation? These days we use the word crisis with a negative connotation when there is a problem. But its Greek root *krisis* simply means 'a decision'; the verb *krinein* means 'to decide or judge'.[1] Today, when we say someone is 'in a critical condition', we mean that they may or may not survive – an inherently negative situation, yes, but one that may or may not have a negative outcome. When we say something is 'critical', we don't always mean that it's bad, we mean that it's very important.

CRISIS? WHAT CRISIS?

In January 1979, Britain was plagued by strikes and economic problems. Prime Minister Callaghan was interviewed on his return to London from a meeting in the Caribbean, where he commented, 'I don't think other people in the world would share the view there is mounting chaos'. The next day a national tabloid ran the headline: *'Crisis? What crisis?'*[2]

I wasn't there, of course, but I'll bet that Callaghan didn't mean to deny that the situation in the UK was bad. Instead, he was trying to add perspective, by pointing out that the British were comparatively better off than people in many other countries. Unfortunately, the headline writer for *The Sun* didn't share the same view – because he saw the situation in the UK from the subjective viewpoint of the British people.

So, when it comes to 'critical', meaning 'important', the key question to ask is: 'important to whom?' One of the most crucial aspects of critical thinking is that it's connected to our subjective experiences. What's critical to one person or group may not be critical to others – hence the poor reception of Callaghan's remark.

Why critical thinking matters to our careers

The subjective aspect of critical thinking is what makes it a uniquely human skill. As we will see throughout this chapter, critical thinking consists of two parts. The first is the 'critical' part, which is where our subjectivity comes into play. It's about the importance of a decision, the importance of the outcome and to whom, the perspectives and judgement and decision-making process. The second part is the thinking, which is an algorithmic kind of logical processing.

Now, does 'algorithmic' remind you of computers? If so, you would be right – computers are very good at algorithmic processing. In some ways they are even better than humans. But that doesn't mean that computers can think critically; at least, not until they can have subjective experience. They can only present us with data and inform us of possible options. They may even be able to detect patterns that are difficult for us, humans, to see. But in the end, we are the ones that have to make the critical decisions, because we have the capacity to judge a situation from both our own point of view and those of others.

Although the term critical thinking could sound cold and sterile in the first instance, it is highly intertwined with our emotional processing. This means that the skills we looked at in Chapter 7 on emotional intelligence, such as empathy and understanding of ourselves and others, can become very useful in critical thinking; as we saw in Chapter 7, our feelings towards a situation can be 'hijacked' by our 'lizard brain'. This makes it difficult for us to think critically, so the emotional intelligence to manage those responses can be incredibly useful – but more than that, the combination of critical thinking abilities and the emotional intelligence to manage them is something that is, at the moment, uniquely human – and therefore irreplaceable by machines.

PRACTICE MAKES PERFECT

From the moment that we wake up in the morning until the end of the day, we make hundreds of decisions. Some are major decisions that can have life-changing effects, while others are much smaller, and we engage in them without much attentive thought. Often, those small decisions are the ones that throw us off our path towards the bigger goals that we aim for. Training our minds in critical thinking will improve our chances of success even when we operate on autopilot. It's a skill that we can cultivate, and like any other good habit it needs daily reinforcement.

Knowing what we don't know

The point of learning to think critically is so that we can make better choices. Now, to think critically, we need to know what we don't know, and recognize when our mind is deceiving us. One of my favourite entrepreneurs is Ray Dalio, philanthropist and founder of the Bridge Water Association, a company that he built from his bedroom to up to 1,700 employees. Dalio says: 'whatever success I've had in life has had more to do with my knowing how to deal with my not knowing than anything I know'.[3]

I think that's a perfect description of the essence of critical thinking; to know that *we don't know*, and that what we think we know is, more often than not, a deception of our mind.

MY MIND DECEIVED ME, AGAIN!

One evening in the early months of starting my own business, before I was able to hire anyone to help me, I was about to go out to an important meeting with a potential new client. I had half an hour to leave: plenty of time to squeeze in the small task of setting my hard drive to back up while I was out. This should only take me five minutes, I thought, which would still leave me with another twenty-five minutes to get ready. I started the back-up and everything was going smoothly… until I received an error notification that the back-up hard drive was full. No matter – it will only take a couple more minutes to fix the problem by deleting some old files.

Have you spotted the problem yet? Two minutes turned into 12 minutes as I couldn't decide what files to delete. Before I knew it, I had only 13 minutes left before I needed to leave. I had to give up on the hard drive if I was to make it on time for my meeting, so I rushed to the bathroom and quickly applied some makeup. Just as I was about to leave, I realized I couldn't find my keys. I checked all the usual places, but they were nowhere to be found. Disaster! I'd let my mind – my mental estimates – deceive me into thinking I had much more time than I had, and the outcome was disaster.

I found my keys eventually, but I was half an hour late to my meeting, and needless to say I did not get that client's business. I promised myself never to let my mind deceive me again. Although I've managed to significantly reduce such incidents, I still need a daily reminder of my critical thinking skills to ensure they stay sharp.

You may be familiar with optical illusions such as those shown in Figures 8.1 and 8.2.

In the first, there appear to be black dots at the intersections of the squares... until you look directly at the intersections and see that the dots are white. If you move your eyes around the image, the phantom black dots appear to move – but of course, this is a static image.

In the second image, the parallel straight horizontal lines appear to be bent; but if you hold up a ruler or another straight edge, you'll see that they are not.

If you simply google 'optical illusions' you will find many examples of this kind, and if you google 'auditory illusions', you'll find many entertaining examples of nonsensical phrases that, repeated over and over, sound like a song, or many other such illusions. However, visual and auditory illusions are not the only examples of how our minds deceive us.

FIGURE 8.1 Optical illusion squares

Image by OpenClipart-Vectors from Pixabay, reproduced under Pixabay licence

FIGURE 8.2 Optical illusion parallel lines

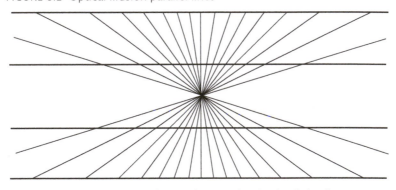

Image by Clker-Free-Vector-Images from Pixabay, reproduced under Pixabay licence

We saw earlier how I miscalculated several steps prior to my meeting that evening, which led to my losing a potential client: this may be an obvious and fairly common example, but people often miscalculate their ability to succeed in many areas of their lives and careers. It's easy to underestimate how much time, energy and skill it can take. Here's another real-life example: every day, we buy products and services that claim to make our lives better and make us happier. But we often have no way of proving their impact; in the current social and political climate, it's extremely difficult to rely on the credibility of any given company. These companies rely on the systematic illusions of our minds to convince us that they are right. Then, too – sometimes even the experts in various fields disagree with each other so widely that it's hard for us to know whom to trust. This shows up in huge national and global debates such as the vegan movement, climate change and the future of work.

So: we encounter these opposing views and claims in our everyday decisions, such as whether or not to believe the marketing claims of a supplement company, or invest in learning a new skill. We also encounter the notorious unreliability of self-assessment when it comes to daily decisions about our own lives and careers (for example, my dreadful underestimation of how long tasks can really take!). Thinking *critically* can help us navigate our way through these choices.

Foundations of good decision making

Good decision making comes down to two factors. One is knowing exactly what we want, and the second is our understanding of probability. Once we know what we want and how far we are from it, we can make a logical calculation of what it takes to get there based on realistic statistics and probability. We fail at making good decisions when we are either not 100 per cent clear about what we want in the first place, and/or we underestimate the probability of achieving it given a certain set of actions.

To understand probability, we need to think statistically. But we are not very good at thinking statistically. In his book *Thinking, Fast and Slow*, Nobel Prize-winning psychologist and economist Daniel Kahneman says that 'we easily think associatively, we think metaphorically, we think causally, but statistics requires thinking about many things at once' – and that's what is difficult for our human brains. [4] Thinking statistically is very labour intensive for our brains; it takes a lot of time and energy, as opposed to thinking with metaphors and analogies, or looking for causal relationships.

Kahneman talks about two systems in our brains, System 1 and System 2.[5] You can think of these two systems as the two photographers in the brain that we introduced in Chapter 7. As a reminder: one is fast but often imprecise, and the other is much more precise but slower. System 2 is 'lazy', according to Kahneman: it only gets involved in our decision making if it really has to. Otherwise, in most situations System 2 happily delegates its duties to System 1. But System 1 is not designed to do this kind of statistical thinking, and that's where things go wrong.

It also turns out that when people are tired, stressed, hungry and generally depleted of energy, they are more likely to run on System 1, which is fast and low maintenance. System 2, on the other hand, requires a lot of energy, nutrients and rest to operate properly. For System 2 to kick in when we need to think critically, we need to be well fed and well rested. Most importantly, though, that system needs to be trained to engage attentively.

The word *engage* is key here. When we see someone who always seems to act rationally, we may think that they are highly intelligent, but Kahneman explains that thinking rationally is more about being fully engaged than anything else.[6] So, the rationality that's associated with critical thinking seems to be correlated with the ability to pay deliberate attention, rather than some inherent level of higher intelligence.

When critical thinking and attention to detail aren't there

When people become disengaged from the critical thinking process, and either a) default back to the 'fast but inaccurate' System 1 thinking or b) delegate all of their decision making to logical machines, with no subjective experience, it can be disastrous. This disengagement often manifests as a lack of attention to detail – this is not the only way that a failure of critical thinking can play out, but it is a common and significant one. Here are some scenarios where things went really wrong at the National Aeronautics and Space Administration (NASA), because the people involved a) defaulted to using their System 1 processes, making their decision making fast but messy, and b) relied too much on technology at the same time. Although some of the best minds in the world work at NASA, over the past decades, seemingly simple mistakes have cost the organization hundreds of millions of dollars and many lives. I would argue that all of these cases are examples of a failure of critical thinking:

- **The missing hyphen:** In 1962, NASA's Mariner I interplanetary spacecraft was launched, only to fail and be destroyed within five minutes, blowing up millions of dollars of investment into the programme. The reason for the rocket's failure was reported to have been a missing hyphen in the computer instructions. Arthur C Clarke later called it 'the most expensive hyphen in history' in his book *The Promise of Space*.[7]
- **Bad measurement:** In 1999, the Mars Climate Orbiter probe failed and was destroyed. There were two groups of engineers working on the programme; one group used the metric system for measurement and the other used inches, feet and pounds. The engineers forgot to convert the measurements when using them, and that caused the spacecraft to fail, blowing up $125 million (in 1999 dollars). One of the members of NASA's advisory council later told *The Los Angeles Times*: 'That was so dumb. There seems to have emerged over the past couple of years a systematic problem in the space community of insufficient attention to detail.'[8]
- **Challenger:** In 1986, the American space shuttle *Challenger* exploded within a short time after launch. All seven people on board were killed. Former NASA astronaut Leory Chaio later

said that 'There was a "launch fever" at the time, to try to get these missions off on time, and get more missions going'. He pointed out that a number of previous successes had made his colleagues complacent.[9] This time, the mistake happened because those involved failed to pay attention to 'the initial written recommendation of the contractor advising against the launch at temperatures below 53 degrees'.[10] It was a very cold day, and the consequences of that oversight speak for themselves.

Of course, not every decision or every lack of critical thinking has such tragic consequences. But it's worth paying attention: as technology develops and we become increasingly reliant on it, the odds of such errors occurring go up. Think about your own day-to-day experiences: have you ever subscribed to a service for a trial period and forgot to cancel it, until you were charged? Did you nearly get run over by a car because you had headphones on and didn't hear it approaching? Or perhaps you've pressed send on an e-mail that you regretted a few seconds later? The more fast-paced our lives become, the more likely we are to fail at critical thinking, because thinking critically needs us to slow down. However, the fast pace of modern life drives us into automatic response mode where we are more likely to use our System 1, or lizard, brain.

Common biases

How can we ensure that we don't default to System 1 and that we engage our System 2? The first step is to become aware of the common biases that our minds are prone to. The list of these biases is comprehensive, but here are some of the most common ones. If you can train your brain to recognize these, you've taken the first step towards becoming a critical thinker.

Answering the wrong question

As we saw earlier, System 1 is better equipped to think 'associatively', 'metaphorically' and 'causally'. All of those ways of thinking are important and useful; however, thinking critically also requires a good understanding of statistics and probability. That's where we can go wrong: we can hear one question, but in our head replace that question with one that's easier to digest and process. This means that we don't answer the original question; instead, we answer the easier one that we substituted for the original. Let's take a look at an example of this, and how we can mitigate the problem by becoming aware of it.

Try answering this question:

On a scale of 1 to 5, how satisfied are you with your career prospects?

1 very dissatisfied

2 dissatisfied

3 neither satisfied nor dissatisfied

4 satisfied

5 very satisfied

Can you explain how you arrived at the answer that you gave? If your answer was 1 or 2, perhaps you thought about how much you earned this month, how your boss or colleagues treated you this week, or you remembered this morning's long commute to work. Did you nearly miss the train and have to stand all the way to your station? Was it raining and you forgot to take your umbrella? All of those recent events are likely to have affected your feelings about your current career path. On the other hand, if your answer was number 4 or 5, you probably thought about the pleasant experiences that you've recently had at work. Perhaps you've just been promoted, or your boss invited you to lunch this week. Perhaps you landed a new client for your company and received a bonus.

If you based your answers on the above recent examples, you have answered a different question from the one that was posed. I asked: 'how satisfied are you with your career prospects?' You answered: 'how satisfied are you with your career now?' If any of those factors influenced your answer, then your brain automatically replaced a more difficult question with an easier one. The first question requires a lot more processing and brain power, and an understanding of statistics and probability, whereas the answer to the second question is much easier and more available in your memory.

In 2015, I asked myself the question in the exercise about my future career as a filmmaker, especially in the corporate and commercial sector. At the time, the industry was still thriving and companies were happily paying thousands of dollars for short corporate films, and social media was at its peak of organic reach. Instagram and YouTube influencers who went heavy on their content in those years reaped the rewards.

However, I didn't allow myself to get swayed by what looked good back then. I started to think statistically and probabilistically. By my calculation at the time, and based on my understanding of Moore's law,[11] I could see that within just a few short years I wouldn't be able to make the same kind of money from simple productions. So I started to remap my business and create a new business model. In Chapter 9 on contextual creativity, I'll look at this example in more detail, but for now, suffice it to say that critical thinking helped me foresee how my industry was changing. Creating a new business model meant that I experienced a dip in the business initially, but I was able to calculate the risk and take decisions in the right direction because I relied on statistics, probability and a realistic understanding of the market. As a result, my business and my career were not negatively impacted by the changes in the sector.

CAREER ACTION – CRITICAL THINKING EXERCISE

One of the ways to beat career fear is to think about your career path critically. Here are a few questions to help you – try to answer the question that is asked, and be aware that your mind might try to replace it with a simpler one. Don't be afraid to take your time, be aware of any emotional responses and do research to help you understand the data:

- How often does your job require performing repetitive tasks?
  - *Hint*: the more repetitive your tasks, the easier it will be for a machine to learn and replicate.

- Do you sometimes find yourself daydreaming or multitasking during work?
  - *Hint*: if you can daydream or multitask while you do something, it probably means that eventually a machine could do it too. The more attentiveness required in your work, the less likely it is for a machine to be able to do it.

- How often does your job require you to interact with other people such as clients or co-workers, to understand their emotions and respond empathically?
  - *Hint*: the more interpersonal relationships your job requires, the more difficult it will be for machines to replace it.

- Does your job require you to understand concepts from different disciplines and connect the dots to come up with creative ways of solving problems?
  - *Hint*: the more interdisciplinary your work is, the harder it is for computers to do what you do. This is different from being a generalist. It's about being really good at understanding multiple disciplines. More on this in Chapter 9.

Overgeneralizing

Human beings have a tendency to overgeneralize: it's really common in System 1 thinking to extrapolate a more substantial conclusion from a small sample of evidence that's available to us at the time. I see this all the time in my work: lots of people, I have noticed, tend to overgeneralize what 'millennials', or 'Gen Z', are like, based on how their children behave. I've met people who are willing to base their entire marketing or HR policy on the mental model that they have from their own kids. But one person's children are – obviously – a *very* small sample of a whole generation! This is a clear failure of understanding statistics and thinking critically.

Can you recognize this type of overgeneralization in your own behaviours and decision making? For example, maybe you've been a victim of crime at some point in your life. Does the image of that memory affect how you feel about everyone else who looks or dresses in a similar way to the perpetrator? Think about your attitude towards your co-workers or clients. Do you treat some people differently because you are judging them by how they look or sound? Sometimes our past experiences cause us to overgeneralize how we feel about certain 'types' of people or situations. But in reality, those 'types' may not exist and we may be creating them in our imagination. Do you assume that certain types of task are going to be stressful, or easy, based on a limited number of past experiences? If you do, you're not alone – these kinds of assumptions are products of your System 1 thinking, and are very common. The trick is to be aware of them, so that they don't rule your behaviour.

SUCCESS ASSUMPTIONS

One relevant example where many people tend to overgeneralize is in determining the factors of success. For example, many social media gurus will tell you that to become successful you need to have a huge social media following. Unless your definition of success is strictly 'fame', there are many more successful people who are not in the public eye, be it in business, arts or science.

We often tend to look at celebrities and social media personalities because they are the most available examples of 'success'. We don't see the many other examples of success in individuals who choose to live a more private life. By overgeneralizing the success of social media stars and celebrities, we may be limiting our chances of success and happiness in other ways. Those individuals are only a small percentage of people who represent success. There are many other paths to success and happiness.

Being impressionable

Here's another trick that your mind can play on you. Sometimes our perceptions – and consequently our decisions – are impacted by prior data that may or may not be relevant to the task at hand. We often don't even know that this is happening to us. Consider this shocking example: scientists Daniel Kahneman and Amos Tversky conducted an experiment. They asked their study participants the following question: 'What is your best guess of the percentage of African nations in the UN?'[12] Before asking them the question, though, they spun a wheel of fortune, and when a random number came up, they *first* asked the participants if they thought the number of African nations in the UN was smaller or bigger than the number shown on the wheel of fortune. When they then asked the 'real' question, they found that participants' estimations correlated with the random number they had seen on the wheel of fortune. Those who had seen a larger number gave a bigger estimate, and vice versa.[13]

I don't know about you, but I found this a shocking observation! And it's not a fluke: Kahneman goes on to give many more example of this type. In Kahneman's example, the prior 'anchoring' data that the participants were exposed to was completely random, and the participants were aware of this. Yet, despite knowing that the wheel of fortune was presenting them with a completely random number, their answers were affected by it.

Now, think about our daily decisions, and how we feel about our lives and careers. These things too can be impacted by these anchoring effects. In fact, to a certain extent we create these anchoring effects for ourselves by the books we read, the programmes we watch and the news we choose to follow. In our digital world, with the constant bombardment of information and opinion, it is more important than ever for us to be aware of the phenomenon that Kahneman and Tversky discovered. Next time you make a decision about your career and life – or perhaps even when you want to make a small purchase or choose a holiday destination! – ask yourself what anchoring events might be impacting your decision.

Seeing stories where there are none

This common mind-trick is related to overgeneralization. System 1 thinking can also lead us to look for a causal relationship where there is none. Human thinking is good at spotting patterns, but we can also waste a lot of time trying to find patterns that don't actually exist. For example, I've seen so many online videos of people claiming that you can 'unlock' a platform's algorithm. Many of them will even charge you, claiming to teach you how to do it. Critical thinking suggests that this is highly unlikely to be a legitimate or worthwhile claim – but it definitely makes a compelling story, on the face of it!

In his influential book *The Black Swan*, Nassim Taleb explains that our brains have a tendency to look for causal relationships and create stories. He shows how the human brain struggles with uncertainty, randomness and probability. Taleb's account of 'Narrative Fallacy' is particularly important to digital natives, since we live in an age of stories like never before. If you think back to previous generations, they weren't exposed to anywhere near as many stories as we see today. Instagram stories, YouTube videos, TikTok and LinkedIn, and all other social media channels, have given everyone a voice, and we've all become storytellers. So, what's wrong with that?

Taleb shares his experience of attending a conference in Rome, where he meets a prominent Italian professor. The professor greets him with extreme enthusiasm and congratulates Taleb on his latest book, confessing that he wanted to write a book on the same topic. He then goes on to tell Taleb that he was 'lucky' to have grown up with his Lebanese background which enabled him to see the world the way that he did. He suggests that had Taleb been brought up in a Protestant society, where people were told that efforts were linked to rewards and individual responsibility, he wouldn't have seen the world the way he did.[14]

The curious and somewhat funny part of this story is that the professor was congratulating Taleb for his book on 'randomness', but he was looking for a causal relationship that would explain why Taleb was the person who wrote that book. The professor assigned Taleb's worldview to his background story. However, Taleb says that when he looks back at his origins, he sees many men of his age and background having gone through similar experiences to him. Yet, none of them went on to lead the kind of life that Taleb did, or have similar thoughts.

There is an important lesson in this story, I think, and certainly it resonates with me. People often tell me that my way of thinking is due to my backstory. However, just like Taleb, I see many women who went to the same schools and had similar upbringing and challenges. Yet I don't know any of them who necessarily share a similar career path with me. I am where I am today, due in significant part to the effect of random events. I didn't have a say in where and when I was born – it was completely random. In my early years I didn't have a say in the schools that I went to, or the teachers that I had. Of course, I can now look back and put a story together about my past, which is true... but it's still a story. That story is not the *reason* for why I am the way I am, and why my career is what it is.

I'm not denying that you can enhance your chances of success by putting yourself in a position where you are more likely to be the right person at the right time. However, the important lesson from the works of Taleb, Kahneman and Tversky is that randomness is always at play and we need to accept its effect. We often hear stories of rags to riches, or other such extraordinary success stories glorified by media and social channels, and it's easy to forget the effect of random events that led to those people's successes. For every dramatic and painful success story, there are hundreds that don't include an extraordinary story to go with it.

SUFFERING DOES NOT EQUAL SUCCESS

Here's an example that, to me, demonstrates the real impact of story-seeking behaviour.

Once I was on a directing-filming job with a small team, in a 'cool' city, interviewing a 'cool' person. One young team member was really excited to visit this city for the first time and meet this famous person they admired – but was sadly unable to enjoy the experience, because they found that actually being there, seeing the hustle and bustle around the city and the star, led to a sense of sadness and envy. They felt they'd never really *achieved* anything. Now, this person was only in their early twenties, which is objectively not the end of the line in terms of potential career success – but they were comparing themselves negatively to their idea of the city, to the famous person we were there to meet, and even to me. Here's where I think they got stuck, though: they believed that my perceived success was due to my difficult background and upbringing, and that it was necessary for people to 'hit rock bottom' and experience 'real pain' in order to grow. Because they'd not had a traumatic past, they believed that their ability to succeed was limited.

Of course, there is no rule that says that to be successful you have to experience pain and suffering, but my team member was not the only person who has seen a story and a causal link where

---

there is none – the narrative of suffering being a necessary prerequisite to success is a common one. To me, this is a sad mistake for people to make, and a strong argument for why we need to be aware of the tricks our minds can play on us. Whatever success I've gained in life has been in *spite* of my difficult background, not *because* of it – and it takes critical thinking to realize that.

Thinking critically about the probability of your success

So far in this chapter we have a gained a good understanding of critical thinking and how randomness, probability and statistics are in play in our everyday life. We've seen how critical thinking is a uniquely human skill, and how being able to use this skill at work is valuable to success. Now, we can apply this same skill to our career planning. Based on critical thinking, what career path should you choose for a futureproof career and maximum success?

Scalable and non-scalable careers

We have previously discussed how to define success – and in the light of critical thinking, and the System 1 traps we need to avoid, let's take that a little further. In your definition of success, is your futureproof career scalable or non-scalable?

A *scalable* career is one where you create something that can sell, or somehow generate an income even when you are not there. This could be a business, where you employ people, or it could be art, or writing, or any other form of product or service that doesn't always require you to physically be there.

A *non-scalable* career is one where you exchange your time directly for money. For example, a camera operator, a surgeon, a lawyer, a plumber and a hairdresser all have this in common.

Of course, there are some lines of work where you get paid more for your time than others, depending on your skill. However, there is often a limit on how much you can earn if your work is inherently non-scalable.

Many people, when thinking about their future plans, prefer a scalable career. It seems to be the ultimate dream, especially when you look at the conversations on social media! However, the truth is that your chances of having a happy and fulfilling career may well be much higher in a non-scalable type of work. Beyond a certain threshold, happiness levels may not necessarily increase with more income. The amount of annual income that sets the happiness threshold will depend on the cost of living in your area, but it typically comes down to being able to have a stable home, and enough disposable income that will enable you to take vacations and get enough rest and rejuvenate.[15] I'm not going to speculate on the exact figures of how much money is considered the minimum threshold of happiness. Statistically, there are many lines of work that have the earning potential to provide us with enough income to live comfortably and still give enough time to rest, travel and attend to our families.

By contrast, scalable lines of work, such as acting, writing, arts, sportsmanship, entrepreneurship or pursuing a career as a content creator on social media, are much more time-consuming. Statistically speaking, you have a few huge stars and the rest barely manage to get by – any one person's chance of success is much less. When pursuing a scalable career, it's important to be aware of the sacrifices that it takes and what your personal values are. Are you willing to sacrifice some of the things that are important to you, in order to achieve success in a scalable career? Most importantly, you will need to do this knowing that there is no guarantee for success in such career paths. If anything, statistically, far more people fail in those types of careers than succeed. After reading this chapter on critical thinking, what kind of career do you want?

Endnotes

1 Cresswell, J (2010) *Oxford Dictionary of Word Origins*, p 417, Oxford University Press, New York

2 Hennessy, P (2005) James Callaghan, *The Telegraph*, 27 March, www.telegraph.co.uk/news/uknews/1486517/James-Callaghan.html (archived at https://perma.cc/7ZS3-YSR7)

3 Dalio, R (2017) *Principles*, Introduction, Simon & Schuster, New York

4 Kahneman, D (2015) *Thinking, Fast and Slow*, Farrar, Straus and Giroux, New York

5 Kahneman, D (2015) *Thinking, Fast and Slow*, Farrar, Straus and Giroux, New York

6 Kahneman, D (2015) *Thinking, Fast and Slow*, Farrar, Straus and Giroux, New York

7 Crockett, Z (2014) The Typo That Destroyed a NASA Rocket, Gizmodo, 26 June, gizmodo.com/the-typo-that-destroyed-a-nasa-rocket-1596004226 (archived at https://perma.cc/5VT4-XH7M)

8 Crockett, Z (2014) The Typo That Destroyed a NASA Rocket, Gizmodo, 26 June, gizmodo.com/the-typo-that-destroyed-a-nasa-rocket-1596004226 (archived at https://perma.cc/5VT4-XH7M)

9 Wall, M (2016) *Challenger* Disaster 30 Years Ago Shocked the World, Changed NASA, Space.Com, 28 January, www.space.com/31760-space-shuttle-challenger-disaster-30-years.html (archived at https://perma.cc/JS4X-LHUU)

10 Wall, M (2016) *Challenger* Disaster 30 Years Ago Shocked the World, Changed NASA, Space.Com, 28 January, www.space.com/31760-space-shuttle-challenger-disaster-30-years.html (archived at https://perma.cc/JS4X-LHUU)

11 Moore's law states that the capacity of our technology will double every two years as the cost of producing it is halved

12 Kahneman, D (2015) *Thinking, Fast and Slow*, ch 11, p 267, Farrar, Straus and Giroux, New York (page number is based on iBook and maybe different in the printed version; please note that the page number could change in iBooks depending on font size)

13 Kahneman, D (2015) *Thinking, Fast and Slow*, ch 11, Farrar, Straus And Giroux, New York

14 Taleb, N N (2017) *The Black Swan: The impact of the highly improbable*, Taylor & Francis, London

15 For a more in-depth discussion of this subject, see Taleb, N N (2017) *The Black Swan: The impact of the highly improbable*, Taylor & Francis, London

CHAPTER NINE

Contextual creativity

In addition to emotional intelligence and critical thinking, here is another area where humans can have the upper hand in the age of automation and AI. Contextual creativity is a uniquely human skill and today we need it more than ever.

What is contextual creativity?

Whenever I speak to AI enthusiasts and engineers in conferences, they are often quick to remind me that computers can be creative, too – for example, when Google's Alpha Go beat Go champion Lee Sewol, some of the moves that the computer performed were deemed even more creative than any moves ever made by a human player. However, that's not the only kind of creativity, and it's not the kind of creativity that we're talking about in this chapter. Just like the difference between 'narrow' (artificial or specialized) intelligence and general intelligence, there is a difference between 'narrow' creativity and contextual creativity, and it is the latter that is important for a futureproof career.

What is it? Well, simply put, contextual creativity means understanding the *context* of a situation, and finding *creative* ways to solve the problem or enhance the experience. It often requires a multidisciplinary approach, and people who have high levels of contextual creativity are often very good at a few different domains. They have the ability to connect the dots between those domains and create new ways of working. So how can we practise understanding the context of a situation?

Text vs context

Let's start with the idea of 'text'. The term comes from the Latin *tepee*, 'to weave', as in weaving cloth or fabric. Human beings were covering themselves with clothes long before they invented writing, and when writing was invented, people recognized the similarity between threads woven into a sheet of fabric and words woven together into a letter or a story. So, in Latin, they borrowed the word for a woven cloth to describe thoughts and feelings captured in words that communicated those thoughts and feelings to others – a text. Of course, writing was not the only means of capturing those thoughts, emotions and stories. Other means of communicating them were painting, drawing, sculpture, music and, later on, photography and film. We can think of any creative output, art form or method of communicating as text: the job of a text is to capture a moment in time, an emotion or a thought.

Then we have *context* – that 'con' comes from the Latin for 'together', so the whole word comes from the idea of 'the whole thing, all the parts being woven together'. Context, then, refers to all of the circumstances in which a text was created. By definition, a text doesn't contain its context – it is impossible for it to do so. It's like being a fish in the sea: the text is the fish and it can't possibly contain the sea within it.

The subjectivity of context

And this is the key: by nature, context is a *subjective* thing. That precise shortcoming of the text – that it cannot communicate its whole context on its own – is what enables us to enjoy a story, or film, or piece of art, because it allows us a subjective experience. For example, when we watch a movie about the Second World War, although the film is about an event in the past, the way we experience it now depends on our subjective experience at this moment in time. As we have seen when we looked at the other essential career skills, it is this subjectivity that makes this skill uniquely human.

CONTEXT CHANGES PERSPECTIVES

Understanding the circumstances in which a text was created will invariably change the way we experience it – sometimes for the better and sometimes for the worse. It depends on how you look at it – for example, a few years ago, I was at the Van Gogh museum in Amsterdam. I was disappointed when I learnt more about how he had treated some of his fellow artists – so much so that my experience of the art of Van Gogh has been permanently changed. I can still enjoy the art, but I now know more about what drove the artist, and I am able to engage with critical thinking a bit more. I'm also able to appreciate some of his contemporaries in a way that I wouldn't have otherwise. This is a clear example of the subjectivity of context.

And there's more. Humans not only have the ability to understand our own context, but *also those of others*. We've considered this idea already, of course – this is part of empathy, being able to consider someone else's circumstances – but this ability to understand context also makes it possible for us to come up with creative ways to either solve our problems or enhance our life experiences. This is what we might call 'narrow' creativity, and when combined with the skill of empathy, it also enables us to solve problems and enhance experiences for other people, animals or even the planet. *This*, as we defined at the beginning of the chapter, is what we can call contextual creativity.

Narrow creativity

Arguably, many art forms created by humans could be classified under 'narrow creativity' rather than contextual creativity; they're likely to be more algorithmic in nature than we might think. Let's look at a few examples from different fields:

- Music: Classical composer David Cope did an interesting experiment in 1993. He released an album that he pretended was written by Johann Sebastian Bach, while the music was actually written by an algorithm that recognized Bach's musical style and replicated its patterns. Many Bach lovers who listened to the album didn't recognize this. Today, computer-generated music is the subject of much interest to the music industry, and many artists and record labels are seeking to use algorithms to recognize patterns in what make a hit song.[1]

- Visual arts: Computer scientist Ahmed Elgammal has developed a generative adversarial network, or GAN. GAN is composed of two algorithms: one acts as an image creator and the other as the critic, constantly judging the first one and triggering it to improve. The system draws 'inspiration' from WikiArt to learn and improve. Interestingly, visitors to Art Basel 2016 found the works generated by GAN to be more inspiring than the human artworks at the same exhibition.[2]

- In writing, AI is now regularly used to piece together news articles. The computers may even be able to fool you into thinking that they can replicate the writing style of any author. All you have to do is let the algorithm loose to explore the output of an author, learning their writing style and recognizing patterns.[3]

All of the above are examples of creativity without the 'contextual' part. Does this mean that we should stop creative pursuits such as music, writing, painting and photography? Absolutely not! However, we may want to take two things into consideration.

First, it may be harder in the future to make a living from the arts if computer-generated art can do a better job of recognizing what people like and give them more of that. Human art forms have often been created out of a sense of pain or of pleasure – being in love, or loss, grief or poverty. AI-generated art doesn't come from an experience of pain or pleasure, but it sure enough does a very good job of replicating it and giving us an illusion that it comes from human emotions. Think about it this way: human art forms have been around for millennia, while computer-generated art has only been around for a few decades. If we can already be fooled to prefer its output to that of real human artists, as we saw in the above examples, then imagine where we might be in a few more decades from now. Moore's law states that computer power is doubling every other year; that will affect the arts as much as any other human endeavour.

Second, to become successful in the creative industries is a statistically rare occurrence. Although today we have the internet and the ability to promote our work to a much wider audience, there are also many more people who are vying to make a career for themselves in the creative industries. In my opinion, at the moment, it is still worth pursuing a career as an artist, since a percentage of the population will always prefer to buy something that was created by another human, rather than by a computer. However, we need to bear in mind that the percentage of this population is small in comparison to the masses. Many people may not question who created a piece of art or music, as long as it looks good on their wall or sounds good to their ears. The reality is that having a career in the creative industries, in the traditional sense, may become harder in the future.

So – is this the end of creativity? Definitely not! While computers may be limiting our competitive advantage in some creative areas, they are opening the door for us in other areas of creative endeavour. If you think about your career as a musical orchestra, in the age of automation and AI most of us need to start thinking about becoming a conductor rather than one of the musicians playing the piece. Of course, each person playing their part is making a valuable contribution. But in a digitally augmented society, many of the creative outputs of the parts that make up the whole are increasingly replaced, or enhanced, by algorithms, and the skill of conducting is one of the most futureproof.

Let's take another example. On a film set, or in post-production, computers can now do a very good job of many of the tasks previously done by humans. In principle, it is possible to let an algorithm guide you as to how to light a scene to get a specific effect that will evoke the emotions that you want to evoke in your audience. So, you may not need a director of photography. However, as computers are closing the gap with their human counterparts in narrow areas of creativity, they are opening up the possibility for us to become more contextually aware and creative in many other areas. Creativity is no longer just the domain of the arts and artists. Today we all need to become creative.

CONTEXTUAL CREATIVITY – A REAL-LIFE EXAMPLE

Here's a real-life example of contextual creativity from my own work. Over the years, I've gained a decent level of expertise in a number of seemingly unrelated areas, for example:

- **Language**: I speak two languages fluently and know a little bit of two others.

- **Communication**: I write, produce video content, and speak to groups and individuals; most importantly, I learnt early in my career the value of really listening to people.

- **Social and political**: I have worked for the United Nations, and went on to study politics and philosophy of science.

- **Leaning how to learn**: The most important skill that I learnt at university was how to consciously manage my own learning.

- **Filmmaking**: My language skills got me a role in filmmaking, and I managed to learn on the job.

- **Business and marketing**: When I started my own business, I realized that I had to market my business to get clients. I started creating content on LinkedIn and won a lot of business from that.

- **Career development**: Thanks to my LinkedIn content, I won a contract to create a video series about career development, which opened up a whole new world of skills and expertise.

The real breakthrough came when I *combined* these skills to create my own career opportunities.

Today, my team and I work with industry leaders from a wide variety of fields. We help write scripts and create content, manage social media and grow individual profiles. There are events, thought-leadership and marketing… and all this work is only possible by understanding the *context* in which our clients are trying to achieve results. When I first started the business it was just a production company; now, it's something new and different. It is creative, but in a contextual way which is hard to replicate with computers, since it draws from several different disciplines. My diverse background allows me to understand many different contexts in which our clients operate. Had I been 'just a filmmaker', I might have never come up with this business model.

When you are building a business, the common advice is to try to create a model that can survive without you. But in the current climate, and with the impact of modern technologies, I don't think this is necessarily sound advice. As we saw in Chapter 8 in the discussion about scalable vs unscalable business models, we have a similar situation here. I call this a hybrid business model, where you have a team, but owing to your unique understanding of the context, you remain the anchor of the business. This kind of business is not necessarily one that you can eventually sell, but it can pay a decent dividend for you to live comfortably. Thinking statistically, and critically, this can be a great business model, much more achievable and possibly less stressful than trying to build a huge business that you can sell.

How to apply contextual creativity to your career

You don't have to be in the creative industries to innovate. All you have to do is understand who you are serving – who is your 'customer' – and how you can get a better understanding of their context. From there, you want to be looking for creative ways to help them either solve a problem or enhance their experience. I often say that the best way to get what you want in life is to help others get what they want!

A huge aspect of contextual creativity is being able to recognize what people might want, if they could have it. As technology enriches our lives, we are increasingly likely to want to go beyond our needs to explore new ways of being and seek experiences that may not currently exist. For example, if you are a surgeon, a dentist, an engineer, an architect or a plumber, think about some of the ways you can add that extra something to your work that will make you memorable and different from others. This is something you can achieve by paying attention to other people's context and getting creative, giving them the unexpected which will reduce their pain and enhance the quality of their lives.

Here are some attributes that can help you find your own creative contexts.

Learn to fail

The number one skill that you need to succeed in finding new contexts is learning how to fail. Be prepared for 99 per cent of your ideas to fail. As long as you are prepared to fail, you will find your way. Finding a context where you can build a unique career and make yourself indispensable is likely to require a lot of trial and error, unless you get very lucky. Some people tend to take the more travelled path since they are afraid of failing. Failure is indeed painful, but just like going to the gym, this is often good pain. Of course, you want to make sure that you don't injure yourself in a way that may stop you from getting back on the field. Failing within your limits of recovery will help you achieve incremental gains.

Connect the dots

When it comes to contextual creativity, you want to be using every bit of knowledge and skills that you have in your tool kit. Don't dispense with anything you know and never say 'Ah but that's not relevant'. Keep an open mind and be prepared to find connections and see patterns everywhere – as long as you engage your critical thinking to ascertain whether they are true patterns, as we looked at in Chapter 8! Look for inspiration everywhere. I often find analogies and metaphors in the most unlikely places. One of the ways in which you are likely to stumble upon new resources is by going on tangents. The 'dots' aren't always found in the most obvious places. You have to be open to learning other disciplines and familiarizing yourself with other areas where you may find inspiration for your work. One way to do that is by developing semi-professional hobbies, for example.

Be an outsider on the inside

Contextual creativity happens on the edge of order and disorder. When you are inside an inner circle, it's sometimes hard to come up with creative ideas to propel your career. I have found clients who were sitting on a mountain of information and knowledge, but didn't necessarily know how to communicate that to their audiences. Contextual creativity made it possible for me to get close enough to their field to understand their context, but I also always listened to them as an outsider. This meant that I was able to push them to communicate their ideas to me simply enough so that I could understand them as a knowledgeable, but not necessary technical, audience. I had to help them come to the edge of their inner circle and take a look outside in order to communicate their ideas with clarity.

Be open to contradiction

Our minds are designed to try to build and maintain a consistent model of reality. The truth is that the world is full of paradoxes, and being able to come to terms with this will help us understand the context of the situations that we encounter. A paradoxical situation may incline you to dismiss what you experience, at first. But if you see it within the bigger context it will often make sense and it can even inspire you. If you remember, we talked about the Apollonian and Dionysian modes of life in earlier chapters. Those are the two most paradoxical modes of life which enhance our experiences and even make life possible. To be able to deal with the paradoxical and contradictory nature of life requires a huge amount of mental flexibility, which we will talk about in much more detail in Chapter 10.

Improvise

One of the most important traits of creative thinkers is their ability to improvise. Life doesn't always prepare us for the challenges ahead and we may often find ourselves in new and unfamiliar territories. In our fast-paced digital era, this is more tangible than ever before. As technology grows so fast, we may not always have the ability to learn and practise. We sometimes need to be able to improvise in the face of uncertainty and use our intuition to draw from past experiences to solve new problems. Improvisation will be much easier if we have more knowledge about several fields. Having a multidisciplinary background will help you improvise more confidently in many situations. To enhance your improvisation skills, try to put yourself in new and unfamiliar situations where you have to step out of your comfort zone. But in the beginning, do so in the presence of people whom you trust will not judge you and will have your back. You can do this to enhance your conversational skills, music playing, painting or any other area of creative expression. Try improvising in your hobbies first before you apply this skill to your everyday work.

Be present

Last but not least, one of the most important aspects of contextual creativity is having the ability to be fully present and engaged in a situation. You can't understand other people's contexts if you are not completely engaged with them. At the same time, having all the knowledge and information in the world is of no use if you can't connect the dots at a time and place that really matters. Having the ability to pay attention and focus is crucial to being able to recognize opportunities for creative input and innovation. One of the most important skills that you can develop is to become a good observer and listener. Being mindful and present in the moment is so important to a successful and futureproof career, which is why we will cover this in the next chapter. So, let's dive right in!

Endnotes

1   Du Sautoy, M (2019) *Creativity Code*, Harvard University Press, Cambridge, MA
2   Du Sautoy, M (2019) *Creativity Code*, Harvard University Press, Cambridge, MA
3   Du Sautoy, M (2019) *Creativity Code*, Harvard University Press, Cambridge, MA

CHAPTER TEN

Mindfulness

As we have seen, to be successful in the new career landscape, we need emotional intelligence, critical thinking and contextual creativity. However, mindfulness is the bedrock of these skills. Without it, it's hard to develop all three of those skills in an integrated way, which is why we will dedicate the final chapter of this book to studying mindfulness and learning how to gain this foundational skill.

What is mindfulness?

Previously, we met the two 'photographers' in our brain, which can be linked to emotion and logic. We saw that one of them is fast but imprecise, while the other one is slower and more calculating. As we go about our daily lives, these two photographers in our brain are constantly chattering with one another. Sometimes one of them gets the upper hand, and drives us in one direction or another. This is all completely normal, completely human and completely fine. However, problems can arise when we lose track of precisely who is in the driver's seat. When we lose track of which system we are using to make decisions, it can lead to unhappiness.

Mindfulness, then, is simply the ability to observe this committee in our brain. It makes it possible for us to see exactly which one of the photographers in our brain is talking, and what data they're using to promote their point of view. When we develop this skill, we realize that most of the time, there is *no one* in the driver's seat! The machine that is 'us' is running on autopilot. This stance is hugely disadvantageous for living and working – especially in the age of computers and artificial intelligence. Here are some possible consequences of a complete lack of mindfulness:

- When we inevitably make bad decisions sometimes, we won't know what went wrong and *why* we made those bad decisions.
- We won't be able to focus on what's important and prioritize.
- We may feel negative emotions like fear, anger and anxiety – and not know why we feel them.
- We may direct our negative feelings towards other people, so damaging our interpersonal relationships.
- We could fail to observe opportunities for creative problem solving.
- We may suffer physical injuries or illness as a result of not paying attention to the data that our bodies are communicating.

The list goes on. In my view, almost every individual unhappiness can somehow be traced back to a lack of mindfulness. Without mindfulness, our brains will work just like machines, running on unconscious algorithms – which puts us at a disadvantage. As we've seen already, when it comes to purely operational matters, computer algorithms are already beating us in so many areas. Our subjective experience is our winning card – and the skill of mindfulness is a way of being more aware of our subjective experiences.

The purpose of mindfulness

It's hard to try to develop a new skill or habit when you're not completely sure why you're doing it. If you are absolutely convinced that a new habit will help you reach your goals, it becomes easier to commit to it. As someone who struggled with a lack of attention as a child, I needed a lot of convincing to apply myself to learning mindfulness. It seemed so hard, and to this day, it's something I have to practise with deliberate attention and intention every day. Figuring out what mindfulness is *for* in my life really helps me stay committed to the practice.

For me, the purpose of mindfulness is to engage and participate in life fully. We saw in the previous three chapters that engagement is a key part of those essential futureproof career skills of empathy, critical thinking and contextual creativity – but it's more than that. People who are fully engaged in their workplace and in their personal lives have a happier career and more meaningful relationships. They are more likely to progress and gain success, because they will be able to recognize opportunities where they can contribute, and help their co-workers and family members. They are less likely to compare themselves to others, or experience feelings of envy or insecurity. In short, for these people, life seems to flow better.

So how can you develop your practice of mindfulness? It's become a bit of a buzzword in recent years, and there are lots of tools, articles, apps and advice out there – so it can be hard to know what will work for you. It can help to understand the science of what's going on.

Three modes of mindfulness

According to Harvard professor Ronald D Siegel, there are three forms or 'modes' of mindfulness. These are: focused attention, open monitoring, and acceptance and kindness.[1]

Focused attention

Attention is one of the most fundamental mental faculties that we possess. When it comes to mindfulness, it's the bedrock of all other, more complex forms of mindfulness, and the one we share with other animals. Imagine a lioness stalking a deer in the wild. The lioness has to be laser-focused on her prey. That type of focused attention is about choosing an object and following it closely without getting distracted in the process. As humans, evolving in the same natural habitats as other wild animals, we also had to develop our attention skills to find food and shelter.

Something unique happened to humans, which changed the way our attention worked. Fire enabled our ancestors to unlock the power of nutrients in food, which led to our brains getting bigger. As our brains grew, so did our memories. We were able to imagine past events more vividly, and construct stories to communicate our experiences to each other. We used our memory and storytelling ability to communicate potential dangers and opportunities both in real time and to future generations. Until then, just like other animals, we were limited by the information that our genes could carry from generation to generation. Being able to store memories and communicate them through stories made it possible for us to thrive as a species. Stories of the past became a guide for future survival. So, our brains developed to think in three dimensions of space, plus the three dimensions of time – past, present and future. The ability to use lessons of the past to enable better decision making about the future multiplied our chances of survival by magnitudes. What was particularly unique about this dynamic was that people didn't have to experience these lessons and stories directly. Other animals didn't have that advantage.

Imagine a group of chimpanzees in the wild; one of them eats a poisonous mushroom and dies. Other chimps present at that moment may be able to make an inference that the mushroom caused the sudden death and that they should avoid it. But they have no way of passing on this information to other chimps, or to future generations. Doing so would require the ability to tell a story. Telling a story requires a form of language, but most importantly, it needs a mechanism, a technology, to 'capture' that story. As a species, we have been able to create mechanisms or technologies of storytelling since the dawn of human history. We owe our success to our storytelling ability, but it has also had a considerable downside for our mental and even physical health. The more we engage in the stories of the past and the future, the more we lose our focus on the present. The brain has only so much 'bandwidth'. Ironically, the only time and place where we can impact the course of our lives is right here, right now. If we can't focus on now, we can't exert any influence on our own experience. This will negatively affect both our present and our future.

Our ability to tell stories and enjoy other people's stories has had a substantial positive impact on our success as a species, but like anything else, too much of it is never good. To succeed in life, we have to balance paying attention to the stories of the past and the fanatics of the future with paying focused attention in the present moment. When we do so, we become more engaged and feel more confident that we can indeed create our reality, success and happiness the way we like it.

Open monitoring

The second mode of mindfulness is open monitoring. It is different from focused attention, where you choose an object, such as your breath, and follow it closely; open monitoring is a more passive kind of awareness than the active focused attention. The primary goal of open monitoring is to become aware of our thoughts without judging them. We then extend this practice to our surroundings and the people that we interact with. Over time, we become better observers both of our inner state and of other people's emotional cues, as well as other relevant factors in our environment. In scientific language, this open monitoring is about cultivating a state of data collection, without leaping straight into analysis.

If our storytelling ability is what makes us unique, then a compelling story has to have a conclusion. In many situations, we might call this the moral of the story. In many stories, the purpose of the conclusion or moral was to evoke an emotion in you, perhaps the feeling of fear or disgust, or maybe a sense of duty or ambition – in order to have an impact on behaviour. So stories might be used to discourage children from lying – like The Boy Who Cried Wolf – or to encourage children to be 'good and kind' – like Cinderella. The emotion was there to stop you engaging in certain behaviours, or encourage desirable ones. Likewise, a judgement is 'the moral of a story', which evokes an emotion in us. Maybe you notice that you are feeling angry – but subconsciously, you judge that anger is an undesirable emotion, and so you ignore the feeling, refusing to act on it, but also refusing to deal with it.

And maybe this would be ok for just one thought, and just one feeling – but the problem arises when we are overloaded with stories and judgements to the point that we lose track of how they are altering our moods and behaviours. We lose awareness of how judgements crop up in our minds, and how they affect how we feel.

Imagine this scenario. You are on your way to work, listening to a podcast about success and entrepreneurship. In the streets, you see a billboard advertising the latest collection by your favourite brand. You are also exposed to hundreds of other advertising messages and billboards, each of which tells a story. As you enter the subway, you are browsing Instagram stories of influencers you follow who seem to be having a wonderful life travelling across the world. Meanwhile, you get a text message from your best friend who tells you she's just been promoted and wants to go out with you to celebrate.

Our minds have evolved to process these stories and extract judgements from them continuously – this is one of the 'auto-pilot' processes that happen without us needing to consciously think about it. Now, every time we make a judgement based on a story, we experience an emotion. By the time you leave home in the morning and arrive at work, you will have already been exposed to hundreds of stories, from podcasts, Instagram stories, text messages and numerous advertising messages. Your mind automatically extracts judgements based on all those stories, and those judgements make you feel a certain way, which affects your overall mood and attitude towards life. For example, you may feel envious of your best friend, you may wish your life was as exciting as the lives of those influencers, or you may start judging your looks in comparison to the models appearing on those billboards.

All of the above are examples of how we get lost in judgemental thoughts throughout the day, which make us feel less fulfilled. The practice of open monitoring is simply about becoming aware of these thoughts as they arise and reminding ourselves that they are only judgements based on stories. More often than not, with a little more investigation and critical thinking, we may find that those stories are not always as they seem and that our judgements may not have been right. However, the first step is to become aware of our thought processes and observe them, without judging ourselves for experiencing them. Once we gain this awareness, the frequency of our judgemental thoughts is likely to decrease. At the very least, we will be more aware if those thoughts start to shape our decisions.

Acceptance and kindness

When we start to gain awareness of the judgements that unfold in our brains, one of the things that happen in the beginning is that we can become horrified by ourselves. People can sometimes think that self-reflection and mindfulness practices are always a straight path to happiness and career success. However, it's no different from going to the gym; you don't become fit and flexible right away. Depending on where you are in your journey when you first start, you may have to experience a lot of pain before you develop these mental skills.

Sometimes things can get worse before they get better. For example, before you start an exercise regime, say, training for a marathon, you may think that you are pretty fit. Once you start, you may be shocked at how unfit you are. In the same vein, when you start mindfulness practices, you may be horrified at how 'unfit' you are, mentally. Becoming aware of your judgements towards yourself and others, or your lack of focus and attention, may make you feel worse about yourself initially – and it could cause you to get caught up in a vicious cycle of self-judgement. How can you get around this?

Professor Siegel gives this analogy: he says that when you see a cute puppy that hasn't been house trained yet, and it poops in the wrong place and at the wrong time, you don't blame the puppy. Your initial reaction is probably to say 'Aww!' When we start training our minds to become more attentive and mindful, we need to think about ourselves like the puppy. We can't get too mad at ourselves while we are in training! The acceptance and kindness practice is a mode of mindfulness in which we not only observe our own shortcomings, but we forgive ourselves with kindness and accept that we are not perfect. Acceptance is the first step towards change. We need to be able to recognize and understand why certain emotions and thoughts occur before we can change them.[2]

When we practise this towards ourselves, we also naturally become kinder and more open and accepting of other people's shortcomings and mistakes. People who are harsh on others usually tend to be harsh on themselves. I, for one, have been guilty of this many times, and it's one of the areas where I constantly have to remind myself to be mindful. Being kind with ourselves and others will directly impact our emotional intelligence, since it's both an intrapersonal and an interpersonal skill. The combination of these three modes of mindfulness can create a big leap forward in our success in life and in our careers. Let's take a look at how we can go about developing this skill.

Practising mindfulness

There are many ways to practise mindfulness; it's just like playing different sports. The end goal for all of them is the same – to become more mentally fit so that we can be more present and engaged in our life experiences. Just like one doesn't have to be a professional athlete to get fit, one doesn't have to pursue mindfulness professionally to be mentally fit. Now, some of us do the bare minimum exercise needed to stay physically fit, and some of us do it rigorously and in a more structured manner. However we look at it, you can't get fit without some kind of plan where you officially dedicate at least some time in your day or week to exercise. Practising mindfulness is the same. The best way to develop it is by officially dedicating time to its practice. You may want to attend some kind of mindfulness and meditation class, as you might for your physical exercise, or you may prefer to do it by yourself. The challenge is to have the discipline to do it every day.

You could use an app such as Headspace, or Relax Melodies, where you will be able to follow a pre-recorded guide. Once you become a more seasoned meditator, you may not need to use a guide. You can focus on your breathing and try to follow it as you inhale and exhale, paying attention to the quality and length of each breath. If you are super-enthusiastic, you may want to join a retreat, but I would be cautious about going into th before you are ready. It's like going to the gym and lifting hundred kilograms on your first visit.

There are also other opportunities for mindfulness training throughout the day. I choose at least one or two activities per day where I challenge myself to stay fully attentive. For example, I may choose dinner with family or friends and decide not to get distracted throughout the dinner, not to look at my watch or phone and to pay attention to the conversations at dinner fully, making sure that my mind doesn't leave the room. I also use this as an opportunity for open monitoring to make sure I become aware of it when my mind flies elsewhere.

Here are some other things that work for me:

- I sit down and meditate for 20 minutes in the morning and 20 minutes in the evening. Sometimes, if I'm going through a particularly challenging experience, it's very hard to keep my focus – but I stick with it. Even if my mind starts to fly, I know that I'm still challenging my body to sit still.
- I go for walks where I don't listen to music or any other audio content. I try to focus on my steps and feel the sensation in my feet as they touch the ground.
- I find applying makeup to be a great time for practising mindfulness. I try to keep my focus on every movement of the brushes on my face and challenge myself to bring my thoughts back every time they fly away.
- I find mindfulness practice really appealing when eating a simple fruit such as an apple. I see how the fruit transforms from being in a perfect state of order to moving towards entropy with every bite I take, and it becomes part of my body. Raisins are also great for this practice. You can get fascinated by how they each look so different.

There so many opportunities to practise mindfulness every day. Whatever method you choose, I strongly recommend dedicating an official amount of time per day to its practice. For me, the 20 minutes in the morning and in the evening are my mental gym time. Ultimately, there are many, many resources out there to help you practise and develop mindfulness skills. I've shared a bit about what works for me – but just like everyone has an individually preferred fitness regime, everybody will likely have a slightly different mindfulness practice. The key is to try a few things until you hit on the thing that works for you.

Endnotes

1 Siegel, R D (2019) The Science of Mindfulness: A Research-Based Path to Well, The Great Courses Plus, www.thegreatcoursesplus.com/the-science-of-mindfulness-a-research-based-path-to-well-being (archived at https://perma.cc/BFT4-SKF8)

2 Siegel, R D (2019) The Science of Mindfulness: A Research-Based Path to Well, The Great Courses Plus, www.thegreatcoursesplus.com/the-science-of-mindfulness-a-research-based-path-to-well-being (archived at https://perma.cc/BFT4-SKF8)

CHAPTER ELEVEN

Bringing it all together

By now, we have gained an in-depth insight into the history of work and its present and future trajectory. We have also learnt about four essential skills that we will need to succeed in our careers in the age of technological advancements. As machine learning and artificial intelligence become ingrained in our workforce, we will be relying on these human skills to innovate and create new career paths for ourselves.

Work has come to define us since the dawn of history; we may not have called it a 'job', or a 'career'. These are indeed new terms by comparison with the long history of work. The truth is that our work gives our lives purpose. It's how we make ourselves useful and feel a sense of participation in, and contribution to, society. Some economists and social scientists have argued that when machines do everything, we may not need to work, and that we can instead follow creative pursuits or entertainment. I would say that the value and the necessity of work for human society go much deeper than our material needs. Our physical bodies and our brains will atrophy if we don't make them 'work'. Well, we *are* our brains and our bodies.

Although there are challenges ahead, there is reason to believe that the golden age of work is only just beginning. We are now entering an era where we can build careers that we can truly enjoy if we develop the right skills and mindset. Work can become more fulfilling than ever. It's up to us to innovate and create new paths for ourselves. The skills that we have discussed in Part Three of this book are at the heart of a more fulfilling way of thinking about work. Whether you are looking to join an organization or run your own business, these skills will help you become indispensable. With this in mind, how can we prepare for the future? Let's sum up what we've discussed in this book; you just have to take these basic principles and apply them to your own industry.

Decide what success means to you

To decide what success means to you, you need two things. First, you need to know your **values** and what makes you happy, and second you need **critical thinking** to realistically decide what it takes to get there. Your values are based on how you view yourself and your place in the world. In other words, it depends on your inner circles, which ones you feel more strongly attached to and derive a sense of meaning and identity from. The second part, which is the critical thinking dimension, is there to give you a realistic view of the probability of success in the goals that you set for yourself.

For example, if your values are strongly aligned with having a strong bond with your family and achieving work–life balance, choosing a scalable career path could create challenges. It's not to say that it's impossible to achieve, but statistically, the probability of building a highly scalable career is very slim and will require a lot of sacrifice. It's what Nasim Taleb calls a Black

Swan event. It's also important to understand that hard work alone does not guarantee success in a scalable career. If you can align your values with a realistic view of what it takes to build a fulfilling career, you are on the right path. The truth is that building a scalable career will require a lot of sacrifice from yourself and often from your immediate family.

Don't discard history, and pay attention to context

Although the past and the future can look very different, history is an important part of understanding the bigger picture. No matter what line of work you are in, having a good grasp of how technology has changed your industry over time can give you a better understanding of its future impact. It's important to see this from an objective point of view and to be open to seeing the reality as it is. It was this objective view of my industry that made me reconsider my business model. For example, one of the most important lessons that we've learnt from a historical view of technological advancements is that the processing power of computers is doubling every other year. At the same time, we are creating more data than ever. Historically, we've never experienced this level of speed in technological advancements, and we've never produced so much data. More data means that machines are learning to do things that supersede human abilities in many areas.

Understanding the historical trajectory of technology in your field could give you a glimpse of what's on the horizon. It's almost guaranteed that no matter how advanced technology becomes, we will still need humans to deal with situations that require contextual input, human interactions and critical judgement. So, it makes sense to gravitate towards roles within your industry that require those skills.

Choose your work culture

When choosing a career path, it's important to think about which work culture you are most suited to, and where you will feel most comfortable. Are you an entrepreneur at heart, stuck in a corporate culture that's making you feel dissatisfied? In many cases the opposite is true. People often start their own business to have more freedom, but the lack of structure that comes with working for yourself is not suited to everyone.

In Chapter 5 we talked about the five personality traits of extroversion, neuroticism, consciousness, agreeableness and openness. Knowing where you are on the spectrum of those personality traits can be a very good guide as to the work culture that you are most likely to thrive in. It also helps to think about your place in the world and where you think you can make the most contribution. For example, if your goal is to help end hunger and poverty, or have an impact on climate change, you are more likely to achieve this goal as part of a large organization, rather than working solo.

Make friends with AI and its human side

Artificial intelligence and its ground-breaking subfield of machine learning are here to stay. Get to know it as much as you can, at least on a conceptual level, and think about some of the ways it can enhance your work and your industry. Chances are that a giant tech company, or a lone engineer somewhere, is developing codes right at this moment that will transform your industry. You don't have to be a coder to innovate and use these new technologies to make positive changes in your field. If you have the right level of conceptual understanding, you can work in a technology-driven environment and partnership in a complementary way. Conversely, if you are an engineer, you would want to think more deeply about the philosophical, ethical and humanistic side of how these new technologies can change our lives and their potential implications, both positive and negative.

If you get to know both the human aspect and the technological side of AI, this contextual understanding can put you in a unique position in your career. More and more companies are going to need to hire individuals who are well versed in both of these areas and who can innovate in how we redefine time, as we transition into a world of symbiotic human–machine relationships.

These tools should be everything you need to beat career fear and make your work futureproof. Good luck – I truly hope this book inspires you to gain the right perspective, mindset and (human) skills for your own career success.

Index

Note: page numbers in *italic* indicate figures or tables

CPSIA information can be obtained
at www.ICGtesting.com
Printed in the USA
LVHW050039230720
661320LV00008B/16